In An Iron Time

Statements and Reiterations

In An Iron Time
Statements and Reiterations

Essays by R. V. Cassill

Purdue University Studies

1969

If truth be beneficial, its semblance is even more mischievous.
La Rochefoucauld

Contents

The Cloud of Certainties   1

Death of the Novel   22

Sounding Brass   27

Teaching Literature as Art   31

Our Unperishing Unpublished   48

The "Too" Critics Smell Blood   52

How Good is a Good Book?   55

The Sears and Ward Catalogs: 1964   71

Tarzan Lives   77

Accusers and Pardoners   82

How Beautiful Art Came to America   92

Looking for an Archetype   96

Friends and Characters   111

Homogenizing the Cows   115

Why I Left the Midwest   118

*For W. T. Couch, who knew the intellect
as a warrior force.*

Introduction

It will be apparent to anyone proceeding through this collection that there is a considerable variation in the tone, the surface of language, and the degree of exhaustiveness in the articles and essays here assembled. Several of the shorter pieces were written as features for *Book Week,* one for the *New York Times* Sunday Book Section. Among these, "Homogenizing the Cows"—which comments on the National Endowment for the Arts and Humanities—touches very briefly and perhaps prematurely on a subject that deserves the broad and patient examination of a social historian with a sense of irony. The review of the Sears Roebuck and Montgomery Ward catalogues was obviously intended to yield some laughs before anything else, as was the review of the Tarzan novel.

Further to explain the superficial scattering of effects, let me point out that these pieces were selected from a body of articles and a small mountain of reviews written over a period of almost two decades. The review of Behrman's *Duveen* was written, for example, in 1952. Some of the longer pieces were originally presented as lectures, delivered on occasions when consideration of a special topic was required. I expect that the reader will find the tone of some of them positively solemn, and in subject matter they may seem only casually related.

But I suppose that whoever reads all the pieces will find them unified by certain major preoccupations. I am writing this preface so that the unity which may be perceived after the book is finished can be, at least, declared from the beginning.

In my whole career as writer and teacher I have been preoccupied with what I take to be the blind spots in the view of the nature and uses of literature prevailing in contemporary America. I am convinced that we have not persisted adequately in face of the persisting question: *What is art?* We have gone on—we go on—as if that question had been sufficiently answered, once and for all. As if the critics had an eternally adequate theoretical answer. As if the practice of fiction writers and poets—the books they write—might be a sufficiently pragmatic answer for a people that still congratulates itself on its pragmatism.

The question can never be answered once and for all. The nature of art and its role in our individual or collective consciousness changes and dissolves and reforms as inevitably as history itself, as Man himself. To those who would or had to listen to me I have gone on insisting that while, of course, we needed fiction, verse, and the criticism thereof, we also needed a "natural history" encompassing both. That we need another envelope of consciousness around those things that literature and criticism make us conscious of.

This book is not offered as such a natural history, but as an appeal to begin a disastrously belated effort on a scale that might remedy the losses we yearly and daily endure. Everything I have to say here spins out from Flaubert's comment: "That which should be studied is believed without hesitation." We study, to the point of exhausted academic morale, the prescribed aspects of literature. We shrink, to the point of intellectual default and sloth, from studying what stinks with the fecundity of death and new life under our noses.

I make no pretense of carrying out an adequate study or giving even a tentative answer to the question of what art is for us here and now. But in selecting the pieces that would be included here I tried to amplify, by example, some of the points I have tired to make within the essays by abstract or general reasoning. For instance in "How Good is a Good Book?" and elsewhere I talk about the salutary effects of the hard reading of "bad" books. The reviews of the mail order catalogues and the Tarzan novel are examples (and only tentative ones, please) of how such reading might be undertaken.

In "Teaching Literature as an Art" I talk about the "reading-writing continuum." (I talk about this constantly as a teacher, too, and make it the basic concept underlying any program I ever propose to a student. It seems an overwhelmingly simple concept. It seems something we all take quite for granted and always have in designing curricula for literary studies. And yet, I have found it bewilderingly difficult to reaffirm, as if in the very process of accepting it we had somehow forgotten it.) To illustrate from my own writing experience what I mean by the term, I have included "Searching for an Archetype"—that piece which so sketchily summarizes the endless introspection and mirror-peeking that precedes, accompanies and follows the composition of fiction.

There is perhaps, at best, only a little to be gained by declaring that a book like this one, put together from diverse and occasional writing done over several years, has been composed in the same conscious, urgent and selective ways that a single essay is composed. There may be much lost by insisting anything at all about one's own work.

It may be wrong-headed or simply immodest to do so. I was struck recently by the comment of an eminent English writer to the effect that he only liked to hear artists or writers speak of their own work when they spoke *disparagingly*. . . .

In presenting these essays, lectures and reviews to such a taste, I might do well to say simply: "These little scribblings were dashed off to meet the random demands of this publication or that, this invitation or that to speak to the academic public."

But such an attempt at ingratiation would have, at least, the demerit of being untrue. . . .

The Cloud of Certainties

It has been suggested to me—I respect the suggestion—that the examples I chose to illustrate the thesis of this essay have, in the past two years, lost their relevance. It was suggested— and I agree—that not only the references to that literary meteorite MacBird but even those to the assassination of President Kennedy have changed their significance in the fevered light of subsequent events, notably the assassination of Senator Robert F. Kennedy. I agree . . . but what can I do? If I replaced these with more timely illustrations I could not do so with the assurance that these, in their turn, would not be dimmed and blunted by events to come before this book is printed.

All speech, all argument, requires time. But we are not given time. We have to seize it as best we can. Everyone knows we must hurry now. Quick, said the bird. Quick, said the assassin. Everyone must know that beyond a certain point of acceleration, hurry itself becomes the holocaust we are trying to outrun. Since I can't provide topical illustrations as fresh or as immediate as they certainly ought to be, I can only suggest that the reader might substitute for MacBird and the assassination whatever he finds shockingly current in the newspapers on the day he reads this. The facts on the front page will be part of the cloud of certainties I am trying to define.

"It was very big to think about everything and everywhere," said young Stephen Dedalus to himself at Clongowes Wood College.

1

A student of mine said to me last fall, "Imagine someone like Northrop Frye thinking about all of literature and reducing it to categories and things." He was so devout in his admiration that for a moment he almost seduced me into sympathetic agreement; for it is very agreeable to agree with the young in their moments of devotion.

Then I thought, in a motion of bitter reaction: The hungry sheep look up and are not fed. I said goodnight and goodbye to the student—he was, as a matter of fact, quitting school to go nurse his talents and his learning in silence and exile, bearded, driving a worn sports car, convinced that the movies were the true art of our time, that Fellini was the heir of Joyce, and that if he kept his eye on the New York *Review of Books* no real evil could befall him as he pursued his task of shaping the (always) uncreated conscience of our race.

I thought: They learn such funny things in school. That must mean they *are taught,* by more than schoolteachers of course, such funny things.

Part of what they are taught is that works of the literary art are autonomous, which is a contemporary way of saying that the reading student may look upon literature or its little parts *sub specie aeternitatis.* That makes him feel like a big shot, for he must guess that truly to see things with the eye of eternity is the prerogative of gods.

And while he feels like a big shot, he and his feeling are in history. They exist in contexts that can be called sociological, anthropological, and historical. If he has learned in school that verbal symbols and combinations depend for their meaning on verbal contexts, then the practical metaphysician will go on to assume that verbal or literary meanings are necessarily conditioned similarly by non-verbal contexts. It will occur to him that autonomous meanings, apprehended *sub specie aeternitatis,* have no relevance to his temporal life, either psychological or social. If he is an expedient metaphysician, as we expect the young to be, he will promptly accommodate his godlike apprehensions to those low, coarse contexts in which they have social value, thus sneaking back into history by the dogma that took him out of it, at no price either more or less than inconsistency,

In a word, the funniest thing he may learn in school is how to gain a historical, social, or psychological advantage by a tactical denial of their contextual relevance to his chosen discipline of literature or literary studies.

"Authors too are historical," says Sartre. "And that is precisely the reason why some of them want to escape from history by a leap into eternity. [But] in each one there is an implicit recourse to institutions, customs, certain forms of oppression and conflict, to the wisdom and folly of the day; to lasting passions and passing stubbornness, to superstitions and recent victories of common sense, to evidence and ignorance, to particular modes of reasoning which the sciences have made fashionable and which are applied in all domains, to hopes, to fears, to habits of sensibility, imagination, and even perception, and finally to customs and values which have been handed down, to a whole world which the author and the reader have in common."

If this is true—if, simply, literature is a historical reality—then a major function of the critic, in his role as teacher at least, is to clarify the connections between the historicity of writing and of reading—not necessarily to think about "all of literature" and reduce it to eternal categories and types, but to illuminate it as a process. In doing so, the criticism of our time would be obliged to find its own meanings within the irrational as well as rational contexts of the times.

(In talking about the "irrational" contexts of criticism, I am not primarily concerned with the dream world. In the *New York Times* of April 2, 1967, Vivien Raynor writes, "A Pollock show to be held at the Museum of Modern Art from April 5 to June 4 will raise questions about his originality, his esthetic debts and his place in history. These questions have been asked before, mainly because his pictures, which were fetching around $6,000 at the time of his death, are now going for about $100,000." Here, in Miss Raynor's lexicon, as in mine, money is an irrational context of criticism. So, by implication, are the educational institutions that harbor the critics who will ask the critical questions which will be exploited for their convertible meanings by dealers, owners, insurance men, and

the museum ticket office. Like art critics, literary critics exist
in a world where their subject is, among other things, an
economic commodity.)

§

Whether or not there is much future in the King business
these days, the young prince (the student prince, I mean) is well
advised to turn always in the direction of his embarrassments.
Flaubert wrote to George Sand, "That which should be studied
is believed without hestitation." It is embarrassing (and/or
dangerous) to study what is believed without hesitation, but
in the long run pays off better than scouting the frontiers of
ingenuity.

I suppose it is still believed—whether or not it is often said
any more—that the function of criticism is to find and disseminate the best that has been known and thought. With the veins
of exploratory scholarship visibly running out, with no more
great scholarly "finds" in prospect, criticism has been making
its ingenious discoveries within the works—inside the museum,
so to speak, rather than by the archaelogical, scholarly excava-
tions that sparked the Renaissance. Borrowing from psychology
and anthropology for insights and method, criticism has had
much that is exciting to say about *how* a work of art means.

But how does criticism mean? How does dissemination
mean? These may indeed be embarrassing questions, but they
are not nonsense. No less than poetry or journalism does
written, formal criticism depend on the mechanisms of language to shape meaning. And surely we understand that the
dynamic of meaning is related to quantitative reiteration. This
is a fundamental premise of educational psychology as of totali-
tarian propaganda; and, as Whitehead says, if you can't think
quantitatively you are not thinking qualitatively. So as far as
literary education goes, insofar as the critic is a teacher, if he
will not study questions of his real as against his intended
meaning and of the ideological climate which his expressions
reinforce or oppose he is simply putting his shoulder to the
wheel of false consciousness.

Of which Karl Mannheim writes ". . . it is not to be denied that the carrying over of the methods of natural science to the social sciences gradually lead to a situation where one no longer asks what one would like to know and what will be of decisive significance for the next step in social development, but attempts only to deal with those complexes of fact which are measurable according to a certain already existent method. Instead of attempting to discover what is most significant with the highest degree of precision possible under existing circumstances, one tends to attribute importance to what is measurable merely because it happens to be measurable."

He is saying, a little more elaborately—and perhaps not quite so well—what Flaubert wrote to George Sand. If it is merely reiterative, so much the better, as preparation for saying that we all know this and admit it when we come home from class and loosen our ties. Individually, privately, we know as well as Mannheim that our disciplines are caught up in a machinery of "false consciousness"—a consciousness synthesized by the coercive power and the censoriously enforced limitations of prevailing modes of thought.

Privately we thirst after the consciousness that derives from observation and intuition. Anarchically we resent the institutionalized disciplines in which we, blinded Samsons, turn the mill. All day long by our systems of examination we measure what is measurable about the effectiveness of student reading, wondering what angel or beast is escaping our detection. Within unanalyzed modes, techniques, and prejudices of critical method we analyze works of "the imagination." (The Imagination! Is it singular, is it plural, is it collective, is it human, is it technological, is it sustained, contained, contaminated by the internalization of institutional procedures? Is she what she used to be?) Publicly we know what to say when we're asked, What is Literature? Privately we stare, stare in the mirror, wondering what we've missed.

§

We dream, sometimes desperately, of affecting a helpful alliance with those sciences that seem most familiarly like literature —with anthropology that tells us mythic stories, and sociology that writes a bastard form of novel. But strictures like the one I have quoted from Mannheim properly give us pause. Just as the rigidities of natural science squeezed the life out of social science, the process of contagions might continue. We have traditionally resisted psychological, sociological, and anthropological interpretation of literature as reductive.

Of course they are. And what is the use of increasing the frustrations of the literary imagination or of critical perception by adulterating them with modes of thought whose built-in, irrational limitations are so clear? We have never been easy with the concept of a "sociology of thought"—probably because we have seen sociology measure what can be measured while it shies away from implications that there *are* things which *"should be* studied," that there is indeed an imperative to go after what "one would *like* to know," that some aspects of knowledge are *important,* are *serious.* However timidly we hide our trust, we have not yet totally escaped the responsibility for cherishing concepts of man and reality to which undemonstrable values attach. Sleep, shriek, struggle to escape—by the nature of our profession we can not escape its responsibilities, the final responsibilities of the word.

But we may discharge those responsibilities badly. It is the sense of what I have to say that in the years since the Second World War we have surrendered them shamefully when we could. Is it diffidence or cowardice or maybe just social impotence to ask, "What profession have we that justifies our claiming the social sciences ought to play a subordinate role in shining the mirror of ourselves and our times?" The plain answer is "a profession of humanism" since humanism almost by its definition presumes a hierarchy of kinds of knowledge, fixes on "importance," "seriousness," and "reality;" and humanism is profoundly involved with that synthesis of quality and quantity measured by the word.

This is by no means to say that the humanist, the professing humanist, will always or preeminently show up as the professional literary man or critic. The professing humanist may appear in the role of lawyer, anthropologist, psychiatrist, politician, or whatever, and out of justifiable anger or impatience with the functioning literary establishment urge the superiority of his science in answering the question that the literary professionals have ducked or muddled. I think that is the situation of our time. I am far from supposing that our literature and literary education have been as nearly adequate to their task as science and scientific education have been to theirs. I am merely insisting stubbornly that the development of a modern consciousness centered in literature was the primary task of the epoch. Literature has not been superseded by any other endeavor that can better study what should be studied or that is more likely to tell us what we want to know.

§

We would like to know what we are and what have been the true necessities, the true realities shaping our times. To know what literature is. And if we never see these things *sub specie aternitatis,* yet our best chance at knowing them is by creating, by writing, a representative Intellectual Comedy (Howard Nemerov's term) and not by advances in a sociology of knowledge or a sociology of art.

Of course art and knowledge exist in a context of irrational social factors. And no doubt critics have tended to minimize the ways in which their meanings derive from the irrational contexts, because to admit the connections would be to admit that criticism has not declared the irrational components of its own meanings.

We are deeply committed to a false consciousness of the interrelation of art and society. And probably just because we are so far gone, science of any sort is unfit for the task of re-establishing coherence between the gross empirical observations we make in shirt sleeves ("They're really selling that boy Pollock") and the delicate extensions of sensibility and method ("In achieving a breakthrough for Abstract Expressionism,

Pollock takes his place with Giotto and Massaccio as a great innovator.")

Science lacks wit, recklessness, subjective candor, and the intuitive gifts of a sense of seriousness, a sense of importance. Without them Man is unintelligible.

If it is to be written—as it is being enacted—the "Intellectual Comedy" will have to be buttressed with gross, envious observations, on the order of the little boy's discovery that, "The Emperor is naked." And . . . just as quickly re-buttressed with the further gross observation that while the Emperor had no clothes, he *did* have a majority of calculating believers who were quite likely to stomp, gouge, and bite the head off any little fool reckless enough to open his mouth and say so. People are not so dumb or so tame as smart aleck children think. They aren't fooled when the Emperor goes naked. They just lack a language for expressing the many considerations that obtain.

Without unscientific recklessness (recklessness reckoned as a component of critical intelligence) the "Intellectual Comedy" will never be written. Industry and intelligence and "imagination" alone will never get us back of the hole dug by great accumulations of intellectual cowardice.

I suppose I am addressing a general uneasiness that comes not only from bewilderment about what has happened—really —in the times of our lives, but also from shrewd and individually honorable considerations of what might happen if the boat were rocked.

The clouds of ideological certainty have opened from time to time. Through the gaps we have seen the iron joints of the irrational working like there was someone running it. No tyrant's face appeared, but maybe an inhuman knuckle or a well-greaved shin. Maybe *something* that simply could not be reconciled with the certainties on which we have based our conduct, thought, and aesthetic joys.

As a minor case in point, let us recall in spring last winter's revelations about the CIA and the student organizations. Anyone keen enough to infer, from that glimpse through the clouds, the magnitude of engineered misrepresentation that has alienated us from the political realities of the last decades would be,

I think, keen enough to note also how quickly the clouds were closed again. And worry about this at home. And bother with analogies between political and literary ideologies. (Did the CIA really subsidize Jack Kerouac in a cunning attack on the novel?) And wonder if anyone else had noticed. And recklessly decide to be quiet about it all and wait to see.

Most of us have a feeling—in whatever fashion we may choose to keep it inarticulate—that the clouds of certainty rolled back for some hours when President Kennedy was assassinated. In our subsequent dissatisfaction with the Warren Report (which was essentially a dissatisfaction of literary critics, or maybe just the dissatisfaction of those who put a copy editor's evaluation on consistency) we surely sense that behind the certainties there are realities we would investigate at one degree or another of peril. Nevertheless, we would like to know—and what we would like to know is not just balanced with "the facts" of the case. *We would like to know what order of importance to put the facts in.* Maybe we are uneasy because of a hunch that the crucial facts have not been publicly disclosed. But maybe uneasiness comes from something beyond that—a primitive dread that the symbols current in our time are incapable of declaring the meaning of such facts as we have—that neither law, political science, psychology, journalism, or the residue of fictive literature can order the raw event of experience. In the political crisis of credibility, when all is in question politically, we may lack the language to ask the questions which would make sense.

If the language is lacking, that is a default of literature, whether the area of concern is one which we habitually regard as a province of science, politics, or whatever. Other disciplines can, but literature can't ever claim that there is any human concern which lies outside its proper scope. Its scope is simply consciousness, and the forms it finds, makes, or disseminates bear the ultimate responsibilities of displaying the relevance of the disparate parts of consciousness.

In speaking of political matters one is not going beyond any proper boundaries of literature or literary criticism. What we compartmentalize for measurement and analysis strikes our consciousness—now particularly, as Marshall McLuhan insistently reminds us—in simultaneous juxtaposition. The language of fiction and poetry is the language of advertising and science and the law. There may be something to be gained by a severe distinction of *genres*. If so, it has already been gained, and there has been too little study of the plight of language common to them all.

In *The Mechanical Bride,* published in 1951, McLuhan wrote, "There are no more remote and easy perspectives. . . . Everything is present in the foreground. That fact is stressed equally in current physics, jazz, newspapers, and psychoanalysis. And it is not a question of preference or taste. This flood [of equally clamorous concerns presented to consciousness by the symbols of the media] has already immersed us. . . . Amid the diversity of our inventions and abstract techniques of production and distribution there will be found a great degree of cohesion and unity."

In arguing that "it is the critical vision alone which can mitigate the unimpeded operation of the automatic" he rambles and skips on to the specification that the paradigm of that critical vision must be the method of Joyce "who studied all his life the ads, the comics, the pulps and popular speech" to expose the "cultural regularities" linking diversities of appearance, *genre,* form.

McLuhan observes that the cultural regularities determine the almost simultaneous appearance of fads, quirks, concentrations of sensibility at middle-brow, high-brow, and low-brow circles as well as in different disciplines or areas of discourse. (Like—if a Freudian emphasis prevails in the composition and criticism of poetry, you're not about to find Jungian mythology showing its face in the horse operas. When the "sex kitten" sells paperback novels, then *Lolita* will reveal inexplicable mysteries of logodaedalic beauty. Corroboration of McLuhan's theory ought not be hard to make. The embarrasing question is why it has not been made.) The idea of an invisible government by cultural regularities implies that if there is a "crisis of credibility" in the relation of the political animal with the mechanisms of government, then that same crisis pervades our thoughts about the nature of art and the credibility of its relation to reality.

§

Perhaps the government has become a work of art, immune from challenges of credibility, subject only to aesthetic measure.* We might then ask in all seriousness whether the critical and teaching establishments concerned with literature have not been both victim and agent of the processes which made "the aesthetic" a clear and distinct *alternative* to "the truthful"— thus preparing a situation in which no one knows quite how or why to demand that a government should be candid.

In another time Emerson might say, "Truth and goodness and beauty are but different faces of the same All." In our time we have been taught otherwise. (I think it has been *proved* that truth and beauty are unrelated.) And if the teaching has accomplished nothing else it has prepared aestheticism as the last refuge of the scoundrel, dividing consciousness to make it vulnerable to the exercise of indivisible power. There may be no tyrant beyond the clouds of certainty, but the throne is prepared and waiting. "Tyrant Wanted" signs are up—and when he comes we can be sure he will be beautiful but not true.

§

Governed by our habitual separation of measures, we tend to talk as if we were concerned only with "scientific truth" in such concerns as the assassination of President Kennedy—the chronology of the Zapruder film, the weight of bullet 399 (or

---

* "Ever since Burckhardt saw that the meaning of Machiavelli's method was to turn the state into a work of art by the rational manipulation of power, it has been an open possibility to apply the method of art analysis to the critical evaluation of society. That is attempted here."—from the introduction to *The Mechanical Bride*. It should be said of this early book that though McLuhan uses art critical methods in measuring the statal and commercial myths which constitute the "folklore of industrial man," these methods are part of a mix. There is also anthropological, sociological method, with the sort of reckless common sense I choose to call humanistic.

was it 369?) and so on. We cling to the safe pretense that our dissatisfaction with the Warren Report arises from its failure to deal appropriately and consistently with matters of fact.

But though we rationally separate the powers of language and will not write the "Intellectual Comedy" that would make their reunion available to consciousness, in fact and before our eyes they entangle themselves irrationally. The comedy is being everywhere enacted, if not recognized or written down.

Here is a shred of it from Jean Stafford's book, *A Mother in History.* Looking upon the wide prospect and the Texas fen, she is imaginatively judging how Oswald shot the President. "I was struck moreover by the fact that between the window and the target there was no obstruction of any kind to challenge aim or deflect the attention, no eave or overhang or tree. The drop shot, from a steadied rifle, was fired on a day of surpassing clarity; the marksmanship of the gunner did not have to be remarkable."

Surely this passage will appeal to our aesthetic sense. Anyone with an ear for the rhythm and resonance of language will grasp that it satisfies certain conditions of beauty. It is neo-Jamesian, Conradian, with a feminine refinement and delicacy exceeding anything we can easily recall from these masters. And how are we to disengage from its persuasive beauty (i.e., its beauty *acting like* truth) when we note that in fact it is not true?

Of course there was a tree. The Warren Report says less beautifully that there was a tree . . . to "challenge aim." Furthermore, a "drop shot" is part of the game of tennis, but I do not think it has anything to do with marksmanship or gunnery.

Since it is a beautiful passage, shouldn't we solve the problem by categorizing it as art and not as truth (or untruth)? Yet . . . the work from which it comes is neither novel nor story, so what right have we to take it as art? Yet . . . obviously it is the art of the fiction writer that we are sampling in this non-fiction work, and as everyone knows from reading or reading about *In Cold Blood* non-fiction is fiction and . . . And we are in a dreadful, insoluble embarrassment over the whole matter, an embarrassment largely manufactured by the dissociation of aesthetic concerns from our concern with what Emerson quaintly called "the All."

The Age of Emerson is no more remote from us, in all that counts, than the time when Ezra Pound wanted to justify the professionals of the word as those who kept the general currency of language clean, sound, and undebased, fit for all the uses of society. As a matter of subsequent fact those professionals would seem to have done more than their fair share of debasing the currency of language, so that one is obliged to conjecture that we will never understand the assassination of President Kennedy (or "what has really happened in the political times of our lives" or other things we would like to know) simply because we no longer have a language or a possibility of language able to articulate it.

The strange career of *MacBird* is a didactic segment of the comedy, a segment whose didactic moral might be *homo fugit*. Or, as Kurtz said to Marlow, "Hide yourself."

I have been appraising and, from my nest in the brush, "following with interest" the historic, sociological, and political career of this literary work since April or May of 1966. I encountered no common reader of it who, before Dwight MacDonald gave the cue, did not read it as a statement that Johnson arranged the assassination of Kennedy. All questions of "figurative truth" temporarily suspended, this, by natural consensus was taken to be the statement of the play. And I think that the grossest common sense, anything short of outright lunacy or imbecility, would have to judge that statement as the most important utterance of the whole.

Then—you all know this, the comedy has been enacted very publicly—*MacBird* was given an exemption from all but aesthetic measures of responsibility. Robert Lowell, who has had something to say about political matters in times past, was quoted thus: "I have nothing to say about the political truth of this play, but I am sure a kind of genius has gone into the writing."

Naturally Dwight MacDonald was given the assignment of putting the aesthetic camouflage on it for the New York *Review of Books.* (I say *naturally* MacDonald, for the intellectual comedy is being enacted by men, not by bodiless pieces of intellection drifting ideally into place on an abstract stage.) *MacBird's* central assertion—whether figurative, poetic, subversive, impolitic, malicious, untrue, or a prophetic divination —"shouldn't be taken seriously for goodness sake," according to MacDonald. Yet, the rest should be taken seriously. As art. Aesthetically appreciated.

In a subsequent issue of the NYRB MacDonald was called to account by a student at Rutgers, Stephen Newman. Mr. Newman wrote, "I do not feel that it is the role of the critic . . . to tell the reader what the author means and does not mean." In effect his argument is that if Miss Garson said that Johnson arranged the assassination, then it requires fantastic sophistry for a critic to argue that she does not mean what she said.

As critic, MacDonald proved not unworthy of this challenge. Rising from sophistry to an extra-literary, extra-intellectual ploy, he produced the author as witness. In his reply to Newman he quoted Miss Garson as saying of his review, "You caught perfectly the relationship between me and the *MacBeth* plot. It's quite true that I said Johnson killed Kennedy because of the plot." We are, I suppose, to infer that what an author (of any words, of any words) says depends for its meaning on the plot he invokes. ("My uncle killed my father." "He did?" "It says so in the plot of *Hamlet.*" "Negroes are exploited unjustly in America." "They are?" "It says so in the plot of *Uncle Tom's Cabin.*" If any meanings can cop out on a plea of aesthetic necessity—in novel or non-fiction novel, in play, skit, or political pronouncement—then no meanings are secure. And we should not take words seriously. But then they might stop taking us seriously. And then . . .?)

In conformity with McLuhan's Law (which says that highbrow fads and positions will be duplicated almost simultaneously in middle-brow and low-brow configurations) Walter Kerr in the New York *Times* based his evaluation of *MacBird* on aesthetic grounds. "Bad verse." (On this point appearing to apprehend aesthetic reality grossly and conveniently different from that which Lowell discerned. The great thing about aesthetic judgments appears clearly to be that they are incapable of verification, incontestable, and, unlike other modes of human thought, utterly unconditioned by interest, psychic factors, or antecedent experience. The aesthetic argument is the modern ring of Gyges, conferring invisibility on its wearer.)

The reviewer in *The National Guardian* (where, I believe, the conclusions of the Warren Report are not much credited and where, consequently, it should be conceded that one conjecture about the assassination has as much intellectual standing as any other) also reviewed the work according to aesthetic measures. I don't have the text in front of me as I write, but it is my recollection that the reviewer found it saucy, piquant, dazzling—a sort of jazzed-up version of *The Rape of the Lock,* except for that troublesome *point* on which Miss Garson found herself confounded by the unalterable plot imposed by Wm. Shakespeare.

And I venture to guess that in the White House, Miss Garson's effort is considered to be "in bad taste."

§

At this point it might be conceded that any reflection of reality which might once have glimmered in the text of *MacBird* has been rendered unintelligible by the purposeful applications of aesthetic measure. It has told us nothing about either the facts or *what modes of imaginative conjecture* could give a tenable position in face of an ineluctable mystery. Well, then. All right. We are rich enough in literary resources to spare *MacBird.* It was expendable.

But what if, in disposing of it to the convenience of all political parties, right, left, and center, by the tacit agreement to judge it only aesthetically—what if the scramble has reduced *Macbeth* to the same level of irrelevance? (*Macbeth* has nothing to tell us of the patterns of usurpation and tyranny in the real world. Shakespeare, like Miss Garson after him, only said that Macbeth killed Duncan *because of the plot.* Such an argument would not only be rationally consistent. More important, it would be irrationally consistent, that is, consistent with what a multitude of teaching critics have been saying about fictive literature in general, for undeclared reasons.)

While I am persuaded that *MacBird* is expendable in our present circumstances, I doubt that *Macbeth* is. For if *Macbeth*, that impure fiction, has nothing true to tell us about reality—and current reality—then by the same token *The Charterhouse of Parma* has nothing to say about sub-assassination politics. *Sons and Lovers* can teach no one anything about sons and lovers. *War and Peace* is mute about war and peace, however lovely the play of language, the elegance of the translation.

When this irrelevance is accepted—to the extent that it has already been accepted and disseminated as gospel—there will be no question of alliances between literature and the social or psychiatric sciences. Then the whole field of reality will be open to science alone. To be sure, the sciences will find evidences of meaning in the literary relics abandoned to them. What importances they will attach to these, around what centers they will organize them, heaven knows.

II

Of course the intellectual comedy of our time is partly enacted by groups, individuals, forces, irrationalities, concepts, and symbols which lie properly in the fields of study of anthropology and sociology. And one finds it impossible to imagine a social or psychological scientist so lacking in general humanistic, common-sensical knowledge of the world that he could not spot the joker in the fragmentary sketch I have given of the MacBird-MacDonald enterprise.

The meaning of MacDonald's aestheticism and Miss Garson's embarrassment about that plot that tyrannized over her like Andromeda's dragon is unintelligible without taking into account their interest. Interest positive and negative. Fear and hope of gain. Miss Garson, to begin with, would not like to have her head chopped off for dire accusations against the head of a mighty state. She would also like to make money from the large circulation and off-Broadway presentation of the offspring of her wit and passion. Mr. MacDonald would not like to have Miss Garson's head chopped off. He would like to put down non-establishmentarian hicks like Mr. Newman who do not know how literature is done in our time. Since he has successfully found the way for others, he would like to play the role of advocate and guide in steering Miss Garson over from the peril and penury of left-wing rebellion to the affluence of the culture barons.

A social scientist would, surely, be aware of these gross elements of interest, but I doubt that they really constitute the subject matter of his discipline. As I have stated them—and I stated them the way I meant to state them—they are not components of an objective world. They are odd mixtures of objectivity and subjectivity. Pity, anger, judgment—in a word, the tentacles of my own interest—cling to them in a fashion that would have to seem appallingly untidy to the scientific mind insofar as it is a scientific mind. Which is to say that, for better or for worse, the terms I used are literary terms, non-translatable into the concepts of any discipline arranged to measure an objective world, as all scientific disciplines are. They are terms that must be used literarily or not at all, chosen to describe events that must be described literarily or not at all.

And the concept of *interest,* itself, is primarily a literary concept—not because La Rochefoucauld, a literary man, uttered a term which must have been commonplace since language began, but because interest has so many delicate as well as gross ramifications through our entire life of action as well as our life of apprehension. And it is the business of literature alone— the domain of language that knows no discipline except its own —to presume a seamless continuity between the gross specifications of interest I made and the most refined that language is capable of.

Miss Garson's interest proliferates out of—before and behind and above and below—such considerations as making money or not having her head chopped off. She *also* delights in the fusions of passion, wit, scorn, and aesthetic release that come from writing such a couplet as:

Bribe, blackmail, bully and attack!
At least I'll die with harness on my back.

Interests are too variable in quantity and quality to be measured by any designedly limited discipline; too hard to express by any circumscribed terminology. The choice is either to ignore them as components of meaning, which is intolerable for any member of a collectivity who is conscious of his own distinction from it, or to go after them free style. That is, to order them by the literary imagination in its critical aspect. This is what I conceive when I talk about writing the "Intellectual Comedy."

It is not the same as saying that the Comedy will be written by critics.

III

Maybe the most awesome component of the "discipline" observed by literary criticism in our time is that nameless mechanism or tacit agreement which suppresses any spill-over of the critical faculty into self-analysis. Literary criticism is spectacularly silent about the interest group from which it emanates.*

While criticism has been remarkably hospitable to selected chunks of Freudian theory and methodology, it has remarkably ignored that phase of psychiatric practice called didactic analysis. In didactic analysis the analyst comes to terms with the irrational ingredients in himself. The assumption must be that whatever the validity of his method it will be reliable only to the extent that the practitioner comprehends the real purposes

---

* There is, of course, criticism of criticism—a rational examination of rational positions, and such exercises have at least aesthetic value. I mean there is no body of rational examination of the irrational components, social, cultural, and personal, that condition theoretical positions, the application of methodology, or the modes and media through which the rational opinion is disseminated.

There is no body of examination. There is not even a language to articulate it. Here the helping hand of sociology and psychology would be required even to make a start.

for which he is exercising it. The maxim that "a neurosis is understood by discovering what it is intended to accomplish" must be balanced by recognition that a *method*, also, serves an irrational quest for social or personal objectives.

How far can we trust a literary criticism that perseveringly sticks to the literary text without any visible concern for its own irrational constitution or dynamics? Why not call an anthropologist, psychiatrist, and sociologist for a didactic survey of individual critics and the interest group composed of all practicing and teaching critics? (Even a simple census of critics might be enlightening if we wanted to find out why certain ideas and formulas are dynamically thrust into the light while others are dynamically suppressed.)

Call in the doctors for a beginning of the didactic analysis. But why not also call in literature, the literary imagination, to analyze criticism? Why does it sound so cranky, so bizarre, so alien to our profession when McLuhan suggests that the method of Joyce is a *critical* method, that wit, recklessness, and the imagination which perceives a "symbolic unity among the most diverse and externally unconnected facts or situations" compose the mirror of the mind without which nobody can "live a human life in the face of our present mechanized dream"?

Why, instead of calling, as would seem so natural, on literature and the literary imagination for its didactic analysis, has criticism moved glacially toward a consensus that "the work of art is mute"?

That is really the question of questions, and it takes a recklessness beyond the reaches of supportable conjecture—it takes downright pigheaded desperation and the untutored instinct for survival to blurt out, "Because they were all scared into it."

Little by little, by unmeasurable accumulations, the word has become a dangerous thing. The critic is threatened from two sides. By the literature whose steward he has undertaken to be on the one hand; on the other, by the social and political world in which he has to profess this stewardship. In the pinch it was expedient to deny the word—to aestheticize it out of its traditional and useful meanings, to objectify it, to declare it mute.

The greatest of interests is fear. Miss Garson is afraid. Mr. MacDonald is afraid for Miss Garson. You and I are afraid of Mr. MacDonald. We will move along with our rational analyses of "the text" because we are afraid to admit—let alone examine —the irrational components of literary meaning in our time.

Auden wrote:

> Lawrence, Blake and Homer Lane
> Once were healers in our English Land.

What happened to them is gloomy, he says.

There have been healers in twentieth century criticism. Richards' *Practical Criticism,* to cite one example, opened a door that showed literature as a persisting engagement where meaning flickered out of the engaged irrationalities of writer and reader. Critics mostly went back to a search for meanings as constants inherent in the text.

I have cited Marshall McLuhan a number of times. The citations all came from a book he published in 1951. What distinguishes the early book from his more recent successes is not the profusion of insights and ingenuities. He has always been and continues to be prodigal with those. It is rather distinguished by a lavish salting of humanistic exhortations to "defend ourselves" against the mechanized dream. These exhortations have effectively disappeared by the time of *Understanding Media.* The message of the later books is: Immerse and rejoice.

What further distinguishes *The Mechanical Bride* is that it sold (probably) four hundred copies. Its influence on critical thinking for fifteen years was very near zero. But now that MacLuhan has become part of the dream, he is selling enormously.

I don't pretend to know who or what suppressed *The Mechanical Bride* and is booming *The Medium Is the Massage.* I assume that where there is an effect there must be a cause. I wish critics would find and disseminate an explanation.

Once, not so long ago, it seemed that Miss Garson might have got *Macbeth* out of the hands of the scholars. It seemed that her writing was a reading that gave it a relevance comparable to that which *Antigone,* say, had for the French during the German occupation. Now it appears she only took it from the shelf to blow the accumulated dust into the eyes of the public.

And so on.

Death of the Novel

Neitzsche believed men ought to die at the right time, and himself withdrew his great mustache from the mortal scene long before our popular magazines picked up his slogan (as they insist on calling it), "God is dead." Now one can hardly pass the check-out counter in a supermarket without seeing a magazine cover that moots the question, "Is He or isn't He?" The topic appears to have the same journalistic status as the question, Can the Yankees ever come back?

But I noted very little response from press and public when Erich Fromm countered with the slogan, "Man is dead." There must be fixed national habits of thought that establish the different journalistic value of the two slogans.

Practical consequences appear to follow from one and not the other. If God is dead, we are no longer obliged to go to church. We can breathe easier about what we have done in Vietnam. But if Man is dead, what on earth are we—whatever *we* may be—supposed to do about it? Go on with our post-mortem routines, surely; for as a Greek with a certain awe of the obvious said, "The dead do not know that they have died."

Nonexistence being what it is, we expect no tables from Sinai canceling previous instructions. No voice from a whirl-wind declaring, "I am not." And if Man is dead, then it seems to follow that there would be no recognition of this through all the inhuman chaos of which we are henceforth a part. Only a universal "No comment."

Be those eschatological matters as they may, we seem to be in a period when much of the literary game is played with equally zippy slogans. A lot of mileage is being got from the declaration that "the realistic novel is dead, dying, doomed or obsolete." I believe that one or another variation of this premise would carry the vote at almost any symposium of academic critics these days. It's a sign of the prevailing mood when a jacket blurb can brag of a book that it "makes an assault on the last bastions of the realistic novel." That brag *swings*—like the title advertised recently on yet another cover of a magazine, "Whose God Is Dead?"

It's probably inevitable, then, that swinging young people will go with the tide. If they don't have an idea of how or why the realistic novel became extinct, they may rest in the security of the fact that only assent—not understanding—is required by those who insist that it is so. We are not in the midst of any great debate about the pertinence, potential value, or the unfinished tasks of the realistic novel. We are, rather, in the midst of a power shift whose ultimate objective is to move all intellectual authority from the individual to the collectivity.

There are broad social, technological, economic, and academic forces at work to reduce fiction to the condition of painting—that is, to transform our recognition of a novel into a recognition of its packaging, a transformation in which the arts of packaging and distribution will replace the arts of observation, verbal expression, and judgment as the elements of value in the novel. (The representational element in painting was reduced to irrelevance *not* by the invention of the camera but when paintings were given more and more the character of huge, framed banknotes bearing the signature of the artist like the signature of the president of a company of guarantors.) For this displacement of value, the "nonrepresentational" novel offers more tractable content than the realistic novel, less distraction from the package value of the cover, the author's reputation, and other promotional or distributive activities to which they are closely related.

Of course, there was a sense in which it was proper to say— as it was being said thirty or forty years ago—that *Ulysses* killed or rendered obsolete the "realistic" novel as that creature had been raised by the practices of Zola, George Moore, the Goncourts, and such. But it was true only in the limited sense that *Ulysses* broke the crust of techniques and conceptions no longer adequate to the sense of reality broadening at the beginning of this century.

Richard Ellmann wrote generously, "We are still learning to be Joyce's contemporaries." But the point is that if some set about learning, many didn't try, being content—as critics and as *teachers,* God save us—to see the great man set up as an endorser of packages that contained less and less operative nutriment.

As with Freud, it is beyond question that Joyce meant to extend the scope of realism and its correlative disciplines of reason. But every great man is a national (or international) calamity. Freud has been paid for by immense trespasses of irrationality. It may indeed be the case that Joyce inadvertently prepared the "assaults on the last bastion of the realistic novel."

If the novel truly succumbs to these assaults, perhaps the funeral games will be enhanced with the ultimate slogan: "Reality is dead." Of course to fling such an absurd slogan on the page or on the air is only to play with words—as Nietzsche, Fromm, blurb writers, editors, and philosophic mankind at large play with words, and as Voltaire was playing when he suggested that if there were no God we would have to invent Him.

"If there were no reality, we would certainly have to invent it." One should be careful not to suggest by such slogan play that reality was, in the beginning, a human invention. It is enough to observe there is no evidence that it was anything else. Believing in reality is an act of faith, like believing in God or Man.

And of course that act of faith is not equivalent to believing that reality was created, enlarged, or kept alive by the realistic novel, or realistic mathematics, or realistic painting, or even by the realism of science or magic. All of these are merely great ritualistic observances invented by Man when the tide of faith in reality was at the full. The decline and demise of one ritual observance—the novel, say—would not by any means prove that reality had shrunk or died, only that faith in it had lost one of its noblest props.

In his splendid little book on Rodin, Rilke notes the multitude of realistic little figures of animals carved to decorate the cathedrals of France, saying that the artists who made them "took refuge in reality from the uncertainties of existence." In any field where realism vanishes, another refuge of the faithful is demolished. That is all we can be certain of.

And yet, in the shadow area beyond certainty, we may discern a fearful ambiguity in Lawrence's comment that "the novel is Man alive." Here is a lightly buried suggestion that if fictional modes of consciousness—with their predication of the intelligibility and coherence of the physical and moral world are dead, then Fromm is right about the extinction of Man.

As to nothing else in modern times, the race has entrusted to fiction its sense of *relevance,* of the interpenetration of quantity and quality without which all notions of reality become unintelligible. Of all the arts, fiction is the one which most broadly connects the homely, private, errant, ridiculous, and immature phases of our lives with the ripened abstractions of philosophy. The type of consciousness invested in and replenished by fiction is simply the realistic orientation of the race to being and nothingness.

I think that behind the fascinating "death" slogans of the moment lies the unarticulated fear that new, emergent and, strictly speaking, non-human entities are usurping for themselves that realistic orientation without which we cannot know or be ourselves, drinking it as fatally out of our individual existences as out of what used to be properly called the human community. To speak of those impalpable new entities as "a collectivity" or "forces"—as I did above—is simply bad poetry. It may be positively misleading in its suggestion that the very strange is so familiar it can be glibly named.

It seems that to name this usurpation and its relevance to what remains human was the destined task of the novel. And here is the brutal point of the paradox that confronts us: Fiction can hardly be expected to report the general inanition which has made its own existence problematic. Those who have shared Henry James's optimism that "the prose picture" of fiction could do literally everything must concede that it hasn't yet. We concede that the conditions for its future vitality are not promising. All around us proliferates the argument that fiction has been "relieved" of its reportorial function altogether. It might be simple enough to demonstrate that this argument is mendacious. No matter. Demonstrations can hardly prevail against the mechanisms and infrastructures that impose their will on our attempts at debate.

So perhaps whatever optimism one feels about the novel can only be expressed in the conditional: Only fiction could describe what has coerced mankind into letting it die.

Sounding Brass

Once in a filmed interview Francois Mauriac was asked what he thought of the film *Moulin Rouge* which was *based*— as we have been taught to say—on the life and career of Toulouse-Lautrec. With a splendid, neck-stiffening gesture of contempt, Mauriac said, "If they don't know any more than that about what it means to be an artist, they might well have the grace to be silent."

But in the way we live now, such silence is unlikely for more reasons than that it is a poor way to turn a buck. In silence we are too vulnerable to signals of awe and dread, the ticking of the bomb, the groans of individual conscience conscripted into conscienceless collective enterprises. These rarely welcome signals of public distress are precisely what the prophetic artist relays and makes audible to the average ear. And therefore it is precisely around the great artist that the yelp and clamor of defensive noise is likely to be greatest, for the signals he brings in clear must be jammed into unintelligibility if we are to live in the social formations that our characteristic media are designed to sustain. Widespread, worked-up "interest" in art and artists may really be the citizen's interest in watching the chains be put on Gulliver.

Such ironies are given intensive illustration by the kind of success just now enjoyed by *Papa Hemingway* and by the baffled inability of its bitterest critics to say just what is most distressing about its content or the facts of its publication. The widowed Mrs. Hemingway finds herself shunted into the same strange anteroom of public incredulity as the mother of Lee

Harvey Oswald—a complainer against the as-you-like-it version of her husband's life and death that Mr. Hotchner is marketing, as Mrs. Oswald is a complainer against the findings of the Warren Report.

Mrs. Hemingway may write—in a small circulation magazine—that she has found an average of more than one error of fact per page in the Hotchner book. But who really cares, since the remaining, unchallenged superfluity of facts adds up to a totality easier to live with than the art and suicide of her husband? And one suspects she insists on these errors merely because it is so hard to make the real cause for outrage heard in the midst of a successful din.

The worst injustice—worse because it is visited not merely on the memory of a man who seems to his widow to have been caricatured into gross unlikeness but upon all the innocents who might thirst for the truth—is that the very assumptions of the book repudiate what Hemingway staked and spent his life to establish.

The one thing most plain, and indeed most widely understood, in what this writer avowed was that the real meaning of experience lies beyond what is visible or what is stated. But for Mr. Hotchner the confessed, the advertised approach to the truth about the writer is precisely that of recording the random statement and describing the easily visible act.

The certainty we once got from reading Hemingway and inferring some of the equation that balanced what he wrote with what he did was that inside the circumstances, behind the quotable statement, biding beyond the facts (which are any tourists's junk to be picked up according to his greed or folly), and indeed "beyond all men"—where a man is alone in his encounter with his fate—there was a *writer*. Surely the evidence of Hemingway's work supports the belief that inside the men's-magazine-Papa there was a sensibility incorporating moral and esthetic judgment fit to measure his own capers as well as another man's, to accept them as one might accept the other incontinences of age, with shame as well as pride when possible, but without misprision.

So justice is eluded when Hotchner dodges past the evidence of the work. There is hardly a matter of fact related by him that is not illuminated—tugged toward a *just* measure—by something Hemingway wrote. But Hotchner gives only the most perfunctory signs that he was interested in measuring what his eye and ear took in by anything he had read. Unavoidably he makes much of the circumstance that his subject was a Writer, but he balks at following down the path of the written word into the secret places at which the bar-room confidences inadequately hint.

How are we to grasp the meaning of Hemingway's mental illness—his blandly labeled "persecution complex"—and his suicide if we will not listen to his fiction? Did he mean nothing relevant when he wrote in *For Whom the Bell Tolls* that Robert Jordan's father committed suicide "to avoid being tortured" (not, in fact by anti-Republican fascists but by the contradictions of a peacetime American life)? It is not pretty to commit to our national bank of memory the idea that Hemingway killed himself to avoid the torture of our ways. But the question of whether it was true or not would persist in the silence if books like Hotchner's did not shovel it under with the corpse.

To write about a writer and ignore the chief points of what he has written is a contradiction so flagrant that it must be purposeful. The tactic will be defended, I suppose, on grounds that Mr. Hotchner's intent was not "critical" or "academic," and that it is the peculiar, mossy, faintly contemptible task of the professor to deal with connections obtaining between life and the literary work.

Such a defense is ironically out of date. In their own fashion and with their own methodologies the reigning majority of academic critics and their teaching apostles are up to much the same thing as the sentimental eyewitnesses to the lives of the artists. The age demands that all hands rally for the noisemaking, the beating on the kettle of whatever discipline one professes.

In his influential *Anatomy of Criticism*, Northrop Frye writes, "the work of art is mute"—which sounds more like a wish than the wisdom of time. Translated out of jargon, it means simply: "A work of literature does not say what it does not say." The poems of Yeats and the novels of James do not say what has been said of them by critics and other explainers.

But once Frye's statement is translated in terms of its intent, as propaganda, it becomes a useful slogan for the dissemination of a new faith. It means: "Pay no attention to what poets and novelists say to you. Let us critics minister to your unworldly needs." Or, more simply: "Buy criticism."

Now to be thus declared *mute* while he secludes himself for the long labor of preparing something to say seems to me the acutest form of torture for the writer. Who needs a persecution complex to believe that this is a cruel intrusion on his fundamental prerogatives? For the poet or novelist who is still upright it means his audience is being whistled away while he is trying to set up his tent.

When academic and popular static coincide and the voices of silence are harder to decipher, where is there for the serious writer or reader to go? How about jaunting off to a sweeter time? Long ago, at de Maupassant's funeral, Zola spoke of "our adored, spoiled brother, dying amid our tears." Isn't it pretty to think of living in a time and place where something ultimately simple like that might be said of Hemingway, who deserved it rather more?

But if such escape from The Age is thought impractical, one saving specification might still be made. You're a writer looking for a place from which to speak in the old way, as one man with something important to tell another? Brother, you're sitting on that place, on your own private flag pole. Just don't get up too fast. You might fall off.

Teaching Literature as an Art

Through a large part of his life Flaubert collected items for the book that was published as *"The Dictionary of Received Ideas."* Into this receptacle he put—along with some other puzzling things—the tags, inscriptions, and mottoes of the bourgeois which seemed inherently ridiculous, hopelessly ossified into such clichés as frustrate awareness and provide popular comfort rather than illumination. Many of the gleanings are "literary"—they show the iron impress of a culture in which sentimentality has become a commodity and humor a useful social regulator. Their naiveté is never natural, never comparable with folk wisdom, though sometimes it is quirky, as if a nearly-obliterated tribal consciousness were writhing defensively within the cramp of stereotypes.

"Muscles: the muscles of strong men are always of steel." "Book: whatever it is, it is too long." "Milk: dissolves oysters, attracts snakes, whitens the skin; the women of Paris bathe in milk every morning."

There are a number of "that which" definitions. "Conversation is that which you should keep politics and religion out of."

It must be obvious that only a very savage man would save up such bourgeois droppings. Clearly the dictionary was one of Flaubert's weapons of defense and revenge. And his title has the curious second effect of mocking the bourgeois mind as *that which receives* ideas instead of doing some of the other things that a mind may do with them. Lurking in the joke of the title is the implied image of the bourgeois sitting at a table with his napkin under his chin waiting to be served an idea as if it were a steak or a piece of pie.

31

Flaubert's tactic of preserving the stupidities of his encir-
cling enemies was nothing very new for a literary man; and for
us, in our time, in the academic life, it is nothing very old.
Most of us came "into literature" clutching the murderous relics
of *Reader's Digest* piety that babbled around us in families,
business, and school during adolescence. "I had no shoes and
complained, until I met a man who had no feet." Remember-
ing such boobosities has sustained us through bad hours and
does more than any positive faith to confirm that we are the
vital remnant in a wasteland of electronic demagoguery,
where Westmoreland's three salutes to Congress overwhelm
argument and the Vice President wraps up Texas with an
"impassioned" reading of the Pledge of Allegiance. We deserve
some pride for whatever distinguishes us from *that*.

But let's reflect that, after all, Flaubert's *Dictionary* is more
than a device for disaffiliating from the bourgeois—though it
is that, of course. In its circuitous, imaginative way it is also
a manner of reading the bourgeois mind, of engaging from
another quarter to find out what the bourgeois knows that he
doesn't know he knows. It is a manner of engaging the world
of power—where we must always look for meanings. It is a
curious hybrid—shall we call it something *written* by Flaubert,
whose imagination, disposition, and selective powers evidently
gave it its form? Or call it his *reading* of the literature and
thought of industrial man? (To recognize that it can be called
either with equal propriety may emphasize an aspect of the
writing-reading relationship which we have almost come to
ignore.)

And it is, in its limited, brilliant fashion, a precursor of
Ulysses and the early cultural criticism of Marshal McLuhan
(to say nothing of how it might prepare and annotate *Bouvard
and Pecuchet*). Did it not lead straight on to Leopold Bloom
and *The Mechanical Bride?*

Be that as it may—and I will return to it presently—I have
found the *Dictionary* a perpetually exciting disturbance. If
I try to laugh with Flaubert (at the dumb bourgeois who rule
my societal life) I find him laughing at me. If I try to laugh

at Flaubert (for his anger at the glacial processes threatening his hermitic art) I find him laughing with me. And I find, always, that the *Dictionary* and its descendants are less a justification for clinging to the received ideas of the academic elite than an incitement to hold them up for reassessment. What if all written history is a mistake? asks Rilke. What if our firmest academic certainties are just the apex of pyramidial error?

One of the most utterly, thoroughly received ideas of our time and academic situation is that painting and sculpture ought not to be "literary." It is, we agree, a corruption of painting or sculpture to force it to tell a story. Most absurd to ask it to deliver a moral. For art is not a sermon. The aesthetic is not didactic. Everyone we know agrees and we agree.

Very well. But what are we to do with this received idea of ours when we try to read Rilke's poem on the torso of the archaic Apollo? You will remember the poem says this work of sculptural art is literary and that in being so it speaks a moral. What the torso says is: You must change your life. *Du must dein leben endelm.* That is very plain speech—however baffling the admonition may be, it is not our capacity to take literal meanings that is baffled. And isn't the whole poem, after all, the plainest possible speech, amounting to a flat declaration that the visual arts are literary, are didactic?

Now, it may seem that I am trying to pull a trick by twisting the meaning of didacticism. (After all, the poem does not tell us to join a party, write a check for a good cause, or shy away from addictive drugs—and that is what didacticism means, isn't it?) But I suppose that I am using the poem as an anchor post for this paper, in an attempt to retrieve a better, broader, and more traditional meaning for didacticism than that which passes current. (And why was didacticism ever equated with the simple-minded prescriptions for conduct that would make it negligible, even contemptible?)

If anyone is tricking you, it is Rilke. Or perhaps the man who carved the figure of the archaic Apollo in the first place. He was saying, You must change your life. And perhaps that will seem trickery to us unless the injunction specifies precisely what we are to do that is different.

I think, though, that we are baffled by the poem (and by Apollo) because it is too hard *on us* to read it, that it requires to be read by a whole man, while we are used to reading as specialists, excused by some of the conventions of our *discipline* from meeting it squarely and fully. We remember that Tolstoy, who must have been a pretty good reader, said that in his late years he used to try, try, and try again to read single verses from the Bible. We find these verses easy enough to read—in a certain sense of the verb—so it must be that there are differing conceptions of what it means to read. And it may follow that the concept, the practice, and the value of didacticism, of the teaching function as it relates to art, will differ according to our ideas of what reading really is.

What does Rilke's poem mean? That is what I am attempting to answer. On the bulletin board above my typewriter I have printed part of it out in German—*Du must dein leben endelm*—because I do not read German and perhaps imagined that I could be tricked into understanding. This paper is another try at reading it—for myself as I try to read it to you.

I am not much interested in trying to read it as "a critic." In trying to get at it, I see myself as a man who is, to quote a friend of mine, "in the academy but not of it." I am neither scholar, art historian, nor aesthetician, and what discipline I have did not come from meeting the requirements for an advanced degree. I am reader, writer, and teacher, and I have to come to terms with the text as what I am. It is as part of my coming to terms with those alphabetic characters on the bulletin board that I have looked for the form that my comments within academic walls ought to have. From my title through the opening comments on Flaubert I was trying to place the Rilke line where I could read it best.

In one stage of my imaginative search for this form, I imagined a purely academic alter ego who would, like me, try hard to read the line from Rilke. This fellow would say, looking into my eyes in the mirror while shaving, "I, I at least, if not my students and time-serving colleagues, take the poem seriously, its moral most of all. Art *does* command us to change our lives. I will change mine. I will finish my book on Melville. I will smooth things over with the department so those who can will help me get my grant. If I go to England on the grant I'll have time to finish the bibliographic part of the job. More than that, to have the students off my back for a year will let me be the lad I was before graduate school. That, plus the foreign air will give my book the wee bit of excess needed to make it better than any book yet written on Melville. After that, I'll write my own emulation, sequel, successor, parody, updating, and variation on Moby Dick. . . ."

Poor straw devil. Maybe it was not necessary to dispose of him before moving on. He will not change his life, because he has misread the poem. As I am still misreading it if I suppose I can change my life by disposing of straw alter egos. The change must be made among real men, among three-dimensional students and colleagues if it is to be made at all. Among real angels. And I must turn back to my proper topic with the admission that Rilke means all art—not just one literary piece of Greek sculpture—says literarily and didactically I must change. Not only are sculpture and painting literary. So is literature.

And what I have undertaken to declare is how it should be taught as an art. On my way back to that undertaking I want to kick one more straw man, or another straw lion in the path.

This lion says: "Of course in our department we teach literature as an art. What else could literature be *except* an art? I have never denied that literature was an art, and neither have my wife nor my graduate students."

I never meant to imply that literature could be anything except an art, but I think that in teaching, literature is frequently confused with books, with print. And print is not the art of literature. We have always to contend—always within ourselves and always outside ourselves—with an idolatry of books, with one or another form of the Great Book fallacy, which always boils down to offering the young a peep at the brazen images of literature and inviting them to worship. Such exposure and such worship have very little to do with the art.

Howard Nemerov points out—or reminds us—what is the right word to use for such a fundamental and self-evident truth? —that books are no more the art of literature than tennis courts are the game of tennis. And he says, "A work of art is like a mind, not like a thought." If this is so, as I am persuaded it is, then doesn't it follow that we are blundering to act as if a mind could be given a simple location in time and space, whether on a library shelf or in some predicated "place" within our restless mental and emotional lives, once we have received it, once it has been served to us like a steak or a piece of pie?

So where is the profit in advertising to our students that a library—or a curriculum—is chock-a-block full of "good books"? What counts is not the proximity of good books but the good and bad usages of books. To affirm this is the primary step in teaching literature as an art.

If the idolatry of books is the snare on one side of the teacher's path, then the devil on the other side is the received idea that literature is "communication." What this idea boils down to is essentially the same as the idolatry of books, for it assumes that the activity of literature aims at delivering something essentially static. Books communicate something out of the library into us—and we rest in possession, somehow having ingested a library, having turned our sweet pink insides into a static simulacrum of a library, complete with shelves, card indexes, and probably a battery of fire extinguishers to use if any of the books ever burst into spontaneous combustion.

The shabby ideal of communication makes one think of a tedious hauling of books from one set of shelves to another. It is a job for a dray man. Hauling stuff out of the book into one's notebook, hauling it out of the notebook to make an article, or to make answers to an examination, which has been hauled out of someone else's notebook. Hauling, hauling, hauling. . . . The archaic Apollo smiles an archaic smile and says, "Don't bother."

What may be communicated (or reproduced) are forms; but meanings, strictly speaking, are incommunicable; and literature is the perpetual production and induction of meanings, formally related but ultimately as discontinuous as the moments of temporal, individual consciousness.

Literature is not communication, but it emerges from our instinct to communicate in somewhat the same way that new and discreet lives emerge from the thriving of our erotic instinct. It is play or sacramental act in which the engagement of writer and reader takes place on the terrain of paper or voice somewhat as the engagement of adversaries takes place on a tennis court, or as the engagement of the human couple takes place in the acts of marriage.

Obviously the functioning of writer and reader are not simultaneously identical—as in tennis one player serves while the other receives. The ball is first on one side of the net, then on the other. But . . . we would laugh the receiver off the court if he received the ball by catching it and holding on to it. We would be astounded if he returned it by catching it and walking back with it to the other side of the net. He's got to hit it back or there is no game. He has to respond with his whole person and his whole skill concentrated on the demands of the moment or there is a poor game. And yet in the teaching of literature we tolerate something analogous to a tennis game in which the receiver or reader or student catches the poem or story that is served to him and either clutches it as best he can or trots back around the net with it in the form of answers to examination questions or as a thesis, a critical article, perhaps, to be published in a "reputable journal."

"When the mind is braced by labor and invention," says Emerson, "the page of whatever book we read becomes luminous with manifold allusion." But the pressures and the very nature of the mass media create an increasingly passive reception of art and thought—a consumption by minds unbraced and unstrung. The question is merely why academic teaching should adapt itself to this trend instead of assuming, for the sake of social pluralism if nothing else, an adversary stance.

Perhaps we should first examine not why we tolerate a lack of meaningful response to literature by students, but *how* we tolerate it. Whether tolerance is a virtue or not, it is certainly the quality of a mechanism, here measurable in the way teaching techniques, the conduct of classes, the designing of programs, faculty, and curricula reach or fail to reach objectives that would satisfy us.

And I suppose that we will often find that a toleration of essentially passive reading comes from a displacement of values in the educational process. The process will always teach something. Teaching always goes on; but the great question is what is really being taught.

I offer yet another sketchy image with straw figures. In this one there is a straw professor who is offering his students a laboriously exact examination of the feminine endings in the verse of a major poet. All over the classroom pencils are busily making entries in notebooks—so, obviously, teaching is taking place. The professor is happy . . . because he does not know that each student hand is writing, "He makes fifteen thou a year peddling this crap."

All teaching, in the family or in other institutions, is primarily the teaching of a life style, of the relation of a person to the materials of his occupation, whether the materials are books or beefsteaks. A teacher first of all teaches students to imitate his own style of engagement with literature. If he idolizes books or if he communicates, his students will follow him a certain distance down these dead end streets. A graduate student in a Ph.D. mill will inevitably learn that one of the uses of literature is to serve, like himself, as fodder for that mill.

And such learning and such teaching sinks us deeper in the muddle. It denatures and discounts literature while "literary studies" prosper.

The positive education in literature must begin with a recognition that reading and writing are naturally a continuum. Which came first, the reader or the writer? Again we ask, did Flaubert read his *Dictionary* or did he write it? (*"Flaubert pensait toujours de son dictionaire.''* Reading and writing are the ways he thought of it, *bien sur.*)

Isn't the writer first of all and always a *reader,* like Stephen Dedalus (and/or James Joyce)—who takes it on himself to read "the signature of all things," including those signatures of other lives that we call books? Is reading a book *really* different from reading a conversation overheard in a train (and explicating it by putting it imaginatively in a verbal context)? Conversely, isn't the reader first of all and always a writer, who must compose in and for himself some synthesis of all the signatures he has encountered in his adventures, dreams, and previous reading? Who can read *Ulysses* as it deserves to be read until he has composed for himself some anticipatory counterpart of Stephen, Leopold, Molly—and Joyce.

How does *Ulysses* deserve to be read? The question must be answered like the question: Does a man get the wife he deserves? God knows; but we have some notion.

My notion includes the conviction that the fit reader of *Ulysses* will have composed his counterparts by efforts of synthesis that include the manual act of writing, among other less visible steps toward mastery of the reading-writing continuum. For the principle that emerges from considering reading and writing as a continuing engagement with alternating roles is that the only adequate reading response is emulation of the whole activity of body, mind, and spirit that produced it. I don't mean literally that only writing a poem is the proper response to reading a poem. There is something different from a question of genres involved here. Perhaps it is a question of responding to invention with invention.

Nor do I mean that a young, inept reader-writer can not begin to read the work of Joyce (though he shouldn't be encouraged to think he has finished reading it when he has turned the last page). But I do mean literally that for a student to write an exam on *Ulysses* which emulates the spirit and tone and effort which went into making the exam questions is heading deeper into the dark. And the composition of a critical article that bows more obediently in the direction of current critical jargons, fads, and conventions than toward Joyce's ways of reading his world is dead wrong.

When we confront student readers, we must confront them with Baudelaire's challenge (echoed by Eliot): *Hypocrite lecteur, mon semblable, mon frere.* Which means, approximately, You who sit there with a book in your hand are not reading well until you can make the first admission that you are reading about someone like yourself, *and* the second admission that you must do something so like what I have done to find and assemble this poem that you are my brother. If you do less, you may fool the examiners, but you will not fool us.

I suppose that we, teachers, ought to try by our conduct and grimaces and daily carriage to let the students see that it is not worth their time to try to fool us. And that it is dangerous to attempt to fool the poet, because in so doing they can only fool themselves.

We must make it clear that criticism of literature is a means of entry and not an end in itself. (When I say this, once again I hear my old straw friend muttering, "Of course criticism is only the support of literature. I always say so. My students always say so. And so does . . .") Once again my straw friend is wrong. Things are not self-evident because "everybody says them." And if we look candidly around us we see Criticism preening itself on the squatty throne of academic empires. It is a vanity that will have to come down.

I think I can, right here, demonstrate succinctly the tug of critical digression. Consider Forster's *Room with A View* and Lionel Trilling's very fine book about Forster. In his discussion of *Room with A View* Trilling says (and I cheerfully admit I had not noticed this until he pointed it out for me) that the progress of the plot is structured on three kisses.

It happens that Mr. Trilling is wrong. There are four kisses in the pattern and not to notice how the fourth one rounds out and completes the action is to miss something delightful and important in reading the novel.

Now—I firmly disclaim any wish to score a point against Mr. Trilling. I remain full of gratitude to him for pointing the kiss pattern out to me. But—I will bet that as you were reading the paragraphs above you felt a twitch in the seat of your pants tugging you to go look in the books to find out whether Lionel Trilling was wrong or whether I am.

That twitch in the seat of your pants—the impulse to give a critical disagreement precedence over your interest in the novel—was the old Satan. It was a denial, miniature but perhaps indicative, that the functioning of the pattern in the novel should be the center of concern.

Of course in trying to keep criticism subordinate we had better acknowledge frankly that works of criticism can be works of art. Who, in his right mind would wish to deny this? Or take any easy comfort in it either? No more than novel, poem, or drama is a fine critical work a definition of a point where we can rest in possession of an enduring treasure or a solid gold bar of measurement. Emerson's admonition that every idea is a seed as well as a fruit pertains neither more nor less to critical responses than to accomplishments called imaginative.

Take another look at Eliot's famous—or once famous—piece on "Hamlet and His Problems." I read it over the other night with a sense of pleasure, mystification, and stubborn challenge; with a sense of having undergone, for my own good, a hairbreadth escape. I felt within an ace of being trapped in a fixed position not worth permanent occupancy. What was Eliot trying to *get at* by saying so prissily that in Hamlet "the emotion is inexpressionable because it is in excess of the facts"? What was Old Possum trying to pretend about the nature of facts? That each of them has its precisely measured little bank account of emotion which may not be overdrawn? That emotion is not, itself, a fact that can be articulated? And if the emotion might be considered in excess of the facts by some arbitrary system of banking or bookkeeping, is not the excess a most illuminating fact to be weighed and responded to in our apprehension of characters in a drama?

I read like a child responding to teasing. I could have called out loud, "Who do you think you're kidding?"

(And if I had, would Eliot not have winked back and called, "Forty love. Service!" I understood he was playing his great game. I braced my feet for the next serve.)

I supposed that this critical essay of his is part of his whole poetic effort. It tells me only one thing for sure, saying as all art does, You must change your life. (When I asked, "How?" the ball came rifling back over the net at me. Some answer!)

If one believed in communication, then he might believe that works of art, including critical essays, could specify how he was to change his life. And there would be no use in that. The conformity would be ephemeral and superficial. Art does not specify how we are to change ourselves, because it does not know us.

By its forms, its allusions, its generic type, and its particularities, it limits and guides our pertinent responses—just as, in tennis, the particular qualities of the shot coming over the net limit the effective choice of the way the ball can be hit. There is no sense in swinging to return a lob when you've been given a low, hard drive with a dirty bounce. There is no sense in trying to read Donne while you're turning Shelley's pages.

Just as an oncoming ball can't say to us players, "Hit me back exactly the way Pancho Gonzales would," just so a work of art—warning, informing, commanding, beckoning—can not usefully specify that each of us shall respond to it with the sensibility of Coleridge, Shakespeare, Picasso, Alfred Kazin, Mallarmé, or Yvor Winters. There is coaching, there is emulation, there is experience, all of which we summon to our aid and incorporate as best we can. But finally there is the ineluctable requirement that each change himself according to the law of his inescapable nature in his attempt to respond adequately to that with which he has engaged.

As I argue the involvement of the writing activity with the reading activity, it may seem that I am propagandizing in favor of expanding programs of writing as part of the curriculum of higher education. I suppose the tendency of my argument moves practically in that direction. But before we come to the point of opening new courses, I would urge a radical reassessment of the nature of the literary process. There is no sense in any curriculum that does not bend to the pattern of reality. And without a recognition—I am only mildly tempted to call it a "theory"—of the way writing continues the reading activity and reading continues the writing activity, any writing programs we set up are going to drift either toward dilettantism or vocationalism. The reading programs, on the other hand, will drift yet further toward specialism, categorical classification, and comma-counting. Our writing students will take lilies in their hands or LSD in their diet, in a dilettantish attempt to be artists without doing anything. Or they will push to "make money in their spare time" as the Famous Writing Schools promise they can. If our student readers are practical young people—we would wish them to be no less—they will determine that ponies, secondary sources, critical reductions are the economical way of extracting from literature all that is required by the examinations of a reading program. Their lives will be changed, but not by themselves—rather by the extra-human forces and statistical illusions that threaten the race so insidiously.

Remember that Rilke's Apollo says, "*You* must change your life." The pronoun is all important.

As things stand now, even the best of writing programs are not integrated with other facets of literary studies. "Creative writing" is a (usually) suspect *alternative* to "criticism" or "scholarship." The insights into his art gained by the young writer are considered unconformable with the precepts accumulated by the graduate student preparing for a teaching career by a "critical" approach to literature—and indeed they often are, they often are.

And there is no use imagining that we as a collectivity of teachers can do what we want without a reliable survey of what we are. Though we teach as colleagues, the responses we make to the art of literature are not all the same. These differences may be complementary, or they may be merely chaotic, part of the babble of the times, serving a reformation that has neither human objectives or inspiration.

The most casual glance at the present teaching establishment shows a residue of sweet old men who say to their students, "If you want to know *what* a poem or story means, you must struggle with it as Jacob wrestled with the angel. You must not let it go until it blesses you."

Yearly there are more handsome young men who tell their students, "You must engage the text with a complete kit of methods, instruments, and preparation that will reveal *how* a poem means."

The sweet old men have sometimes not got around to telling their students very much about how to wrestle with angels. The handsome young men sometimes convey the impression that there is no such thing as an angel to be wrestled with.

If there were a simple, partisan choice to be made between the proponents of *what* and *how,* I would surely take my stand with the sweet old men. Without a sustaining faith that meaning is the objective of the literary activity, why bother with it?

But since literature exists in a temporal and historic world —in spite of all attempts to spatialize it or aestheticize it into eternity—a third major question resides in the literary experience: *When* does a poem mean?

> What does a poem mean?
> How does a poem mean?
> When does a poem mean?

I find in this triad of questions a promise of high and low enlightenment that none of them offers alone; though, of course, it is impossible to answer the third one well without engaging the others. I am in no sense arguing for the abolition of any techniques of teaching now practiced. I am, before anything else, urging a comprehensive view that would justify all these techniques by emphasizing the multiform communion of which they are properly a part.

A poem or story means when someone makes it mean. As far as I can tell it does not go on meaning evenly and consistently by itself when it is not engaged—like a forgotten light shining away in the closet of a house deserted for the weekend. Whoever found, or could find, that the meaning of literature was a mechanical current shining forth a constant charge of significance? It is not on tap. Nor is it automatic. The energy which is a part of meaning isn't and can't be in the text.

When does Apollo speak? When Rilke makes him speak. When does Rilke speak? When we make him speak. And he means what Apollo means when we make him mean that. Not evenly or every day, perhaps.

I don't suppose that I am claiming anything inconsistent with common experience when I say that *among* the times when I make a story, or poem, or dictionary of received ideas mean something are the times when I am writing in response to them, when I wrestle with someone else's text over or beside (below, behind) my typewriter; when I try to talk about it with students; when I try to make it bless or support a story, or novel, or article for which I have borrowed it. Or when I remember that it takes two to dance and shuffle into its embrace to dance with it.

Not a poet, I find myself engaged with poetry—and in my own terms, *reading* it as I write. Occasionally on the surface of what I write, in bits and pieces and occasionally correct quotation, poetry appears as borrowing or a claiming. (Is poetry Baudelaire's because he wrote it? Or mine because I am reading it? Am I reading from a book what Baudelaire read elsewhere when I write into my text something that he published over his signature?) These real questions will not answer themselves. You will answer them with your own meanings.

For myself I will say that there are some lines of Baudelaire that I keep trying to read as I write. The appearance of these lines in my work is testimony that somewhere out of sight I have made them mean something. There are lines of Rilke that I am trying to read. There is the smile of the archaic Apollo that I am trying to read. . . . Do you read me, *hypocrite lecteur?*

Once, as part of a persisting effort to read D. H. Lawrence's "Rocking Horse Winner," I wrote an imitation of it called "The War in the Air." While I was writing it I was making Lawrence's story mean.

Recently I have been talking about Lawrence's story with undergraduate students. *Then* I was making it mean. For myself. I could only make it mean for myself. There is no communication of meanings from me to them, though they may learn to imitate the gestures and form of my ways of reading. After that, each of them in his dark lonesome must make it mean for himself, when and as he can.

To recognize such limits is not to minimize the authority of the art of literature. It only reduces the false aggrandizement that has separated literature and literary studies from the experience and intuition of the world. It is not to say that every student of literature must be a professed or professional writer, but only to underline that reading not braced by labor and invention is a people-killing time killer.

And it is to suggest a view of literature that might open up again a window between the classroom and the sidewalk, between the academic elite and their besiegers. It suggests a way of teaching Flaubert (and then Joyce, and then the other great readers of the times and the modern consciousness) which does not emphasize alienation any more than engagement.

Once when Flaubert was reading the great book of bourgeois commonplaces and selecting from it for his dictionary, he said, "I could demonstrate in it that the majorities are always right, the minorities always wrong."

Of course he was being ironic to the point of crudeness when he wrote that. But we mustn't understand him too quickly. The dictionary is a many-edged blade without a handle. And as we try to make his irony mean its best for us, which way should we construe it?

Why should we not say, as teachers—*critics*—that in reading Flaubert, Joyce came to read not the unique accomplishment of a unique sensibility, but the commonplaces in which wisdom and poetry so bafflingly hide and reveal themselves? I think that in learning to read *as* (not *what*) Flaubert read, Joyce passed over from the alienated minority in which he and his character Stephen Dedalus had taken priggish refuge for so long and began to read the wisdom of the majority, which he copied down to represent the vast, fictive mind of Leopold Bloom.

Why shouldn't we proclaim, even in the dry air of the classroom, that the great readers will always be great writers, whether their medium is prose or poetry or the little pencil marks a great student makes on the silly objective tests we give him.

Those of us involved with literary education are perhaps luckily placed to see that reading and writing are two sides of the same coin. In seeing this we ought reverently to remember what every hod carrier knows: that when you lay a coin on the counter to buy a glass of beer you spend both sides at once. Why neglect what hod carriers know when we come to designing a curriculum?

Indeed it may always be practical to separate classes in reading and writing in any given program of study. We can still make clear that in spite of provisional separations these separated classes develop the same activity.

In reading, as in continuing to write American literature, we can affirm that by their publications American writers are still trying to read Whitman—who said among other baffling utterances: "I swear I begin to see the meaning of these things."

As we read that better, by our writing, teaching, or whatever, we come nearer to the point where we can read well what Tolstoy meant when he said that telling a story was like joining hands in a ring, with the teacher's hands held on either side by the hands of his students.

Reading Tolstoy well, we read Rilke better, and when we read Rilke better, we have a better chance of reading what the archaic Apollo says.

Our Unperishing Unpublished

There are more writers in this country than anyone dares admit. It is my tremulous prediction that from here on out the increase of their numbers will outpace automation. They rise like guerrillas from the population at large, breaking cover from Federal penitentiaries and the faculties of junior colleges. The vocation breaks out among counselors at youth camps as well as in the shadows of the Algonquin, from the spiritual slums of disillusioned sports fandom as well as among the readers-from-childhood. The writing army is young and old, firm and halt, aggressive and patient, self-advertising and reclusive. Some writers are famous (a few); and some (even fewer) are known only to God. The majority is placed in the spectrum of recognition by their families, at least. ("Dear Son, Your mother stopped off in Honolulu to work on her novel. I am continuing cruise.")

On the evidence—partially suppressed by the Top Dogs—there are a myriad of American poets known at least to the local or regional poetry club. Only a fraction of the writing horde is known by New York agents or the first readers at publishing houses. A fraction of this fraction is known to readers of book reviews. Only a symbolic handful is known by the nation. With a sort of willful Bourbon blindness, the nation pretends there are no writers except very famous ones.

Good people with responsibilities to the book trade understand pragmatically that they and their enterprise would be swept away in the rush if they did not deny the epithet of "writer" to all those who cannot be successfully marketed. In loyalty to these good people, I ought to be making fun of all "the old ladies and nuts" who are at this instant turning out fiction, drama, and verse. You will see that I am not going to do any such thing. My loyalties are pretty divided; a literary Talleyrand at heart, I can jump either way.

On the ramparts of the Bourbon definition of our literature we find the mass of academic critics. Guardians of "the best," they try to skim the cream of the ages and ignore the milk on which it rose. They admit only a few "writers" in our poor age. In support of such critics, one numbers the lumpen cynics encountered in club cars who leer and ask, "Yuh writer, huh? Published anything?"—and then affect an overwhelming dismissal by letting it be known they never heard of one's titles. (Sometimes when trapped by such hostiles I admit that I wrote *The Wasteland* and *Ulysses*. Doesn't help a bit. They *still* never heard of me.)

But neither Bourbon nor Philistine denials change anything. We are writers—Auden and I and Lash Paynter (*nom de plume*) of West Waco, Texas. John O'Hara and I and Miniver C. Hogan, who brings a new story to me for criticism each month. *We* know we are writers. And what does degree or extent of public recognition matter against those recognitions in the mirror where one sees the unique profundity of his own eyes and admits, "I am a writer!" The culture may pretend our non-existence because it has no fit way to house us. That, of course, will have to be corrected. Which won't be easy.

It has been a long while since Whitman proclaimed with satisfaction that he heard America singing. Those of us who, in our time, hear on the night wind the incessant, rising hammer of American typewriters are racked with foreboding. "This question, like a fire bell in the night, fills me with terror." For, by our inherited definition of The Writer, each one of them writes for the race and for eternity. Just as much as Goethe, young Miniver Hogan has it in him to ask, "Do I live while others live?"

Hemingway said truly that writers are like wolves. Through my teaching I am constantly in contact with young writers whose positively anarchic generosity is crossed in each with a wolfish determination to be *the* writer of his generation. What would become of any of them if they guessed too soon how many times their determination to be unique is exactly duplicated among their fellow wolves?

One sees the ghastly contradictions ahead for each writer setting out, for all of them setting out determined to put all their feet in the same footprints at the same time. And yet one honors and encourages their writing because it is so apparent that the best in them thrives when they are functioning as writers. "Behold yon simpering dame" at a writers' conference with a sheaf of poems in her hand and half a novel in the trunk of her Cadillac. By George, at least she's a better woman while she's trying to recapture the past in her novel than most of the rest of the time. She knows it too, and you've got to respect that knowledge even though the instinct of self-preservation makes you refuse to read her product.

Behold, too, the gifted and intelligent young people who come to places like the Writers Workshop at the U of Iowa. A great many of them succeed brilliantly in the academic English programs that they take concurrently with their projects in fiction or verse. Yet, to my knowledge, there has not been one of them over the years who did not hold his scholarly accomplishments in scorn compared to his frequently unrewarded efforts as a writer. Their best efforts may abort—for a multitude of reasons, inherent and external. Nevertheless their humanity rides with those best efforts, and a culture that lacks the means to recognize this is incompletely human.

How shall we recognize it? Oh my, I don't know. I only know the horde of American writers and the mass of American writing will never be matched by a readership in proportions that we think constitute successful literary communication.

Sometimes I have a strange image of a new sort of library emerging to match the need. This library will have no loan desks. Reading will be prohibited on the premises. The stacks will be closed. But these edifices will serve as repositories for all aborted works, all first drafts, notebooks, sketches, lousy projections of great conceptions, and unused observations from life prepared by *all* the writers in the country, however many of them there turn out to be.

Such libraries would contain the Unknown American Literature. As we passed their windowless facades, we could at least lift our hats in salute. Each of us might realize that the paltry list of books he reads each year is only the shadow of a vast defiance hurled at the Void we could not conquer.

The 'Too' Critics Smell Blood

Since systematic criticism of literature began, it has been notorious that a "system" provided a fine smoke screen behind which to advance the prejudices of bias, group interest, or plain insensitivity. The more cumbersome and jargonistic the system, the better the chance for a critical priesthood to prosper by blowing it in the eyes of the unwary, young and old. Give an academic confidence man "sublimity," "organic form," or "the principle of elegance" as the blue ribbons for literary merit and the first thing you know he's hung them on the necks of his cronies or old favorites. Let an academic explicator really haul off on the world-inclusive symbolism of *Lord of the Flies* and the next thing you know you've got a bunch of indoctrinated students telling you there's never been but one sex of human-kind and that one is English schoolboys.

Living in an "age of criticism"—as the vocational critics insist we do, though happily not everyone has noticed this—a person of naturally jaundiced eye is bound to note some pretty yellow maneuvers by the successive generations of Neo-New Critics. At the most innocent, critics do such things as making out that *Man's Fate* is not, oh, certainly not, a "Communist novel"—probably because they like it and want to go on teaching it to their classes without the embarrassment of inquisition by some hypothetical watchdog committee. The only cost of interpreting it as non-Communist is to make it unintelligible, and by extension to make Malraux's career unintelligible and the Thirties as remote and inaccessible as Babylon. And who cares about that? Who cares if the Johnnies in graduate school can't read contemporary fiction or history properly as long as they are being shaped into a consumer market for proliferating books of criticism? It is true, of course, that Gresham's Law works in literature as well as finance. Bad money drives out good, and we may yet find ourselves in an "age of criticism."

A bit less innocent is the critic's boondoggle of discovering that long established works mean something diametrically different from what they have always been thought to mean. Did you know that Iago was the existential hero of *Othello*? That the "abominations" attributed to Kurtz in *The Heart of Darkness* are really Kierkegaardian leaps of faith? That Raskolnikov killed the old pawnbroker so he would be punished? Discoveries of this sort cause quite a flurry in the academic hen roosts. In Hollywood they would be recognized as *treatments*— i.e., the adulteration of famous works to make them more conformable to slovenly or fashionable morality.

It seems to me, however, that the "age of criticism" will not be fully achieved by cumbersome academic systems. They don't finally provide enough bang for the buck. They are analogous to our present fission-fusion-fission hardware, which, as we know, will become obsolete the day some Dyak invents a two-dollar disintegrator powered by dry cells. Just so, "too" criticism will accomplish the ends of a lot of new critical strategy at a fantastic fraction of the investments and preparation.

"Too" criticism consists, obviously, of a single, simple verbal trick as ancient as cunning, its effectiveness depending on timing and the milieu in which it is employed. I am only concerned with pointing out where, according to Gresham's Law, it fits into the cycle of academic progress.

A few years ago I became aware of a new type of professional student—not the classic type who happened to like college life so well he refused to take his degree and go, but instead accumulated hundreds of hours of credit and switched majors and entrenched himself as a molder of opinion in the academic underworld.

The young lady I encountered streamlined all this by coming to our university and setting up as junior sibyl and professional student without bothering to matriculate at all. She was just here, nursing the intellectual powers she withheld from the taint of the classroom, overwhelming the editors of the student newspaper with her news from nowhere, and—for the benefit of her art-minded coterie—practicing "too" criticism on theater, painting, and literature.

I sat in the sibylline presence a couple of times and heard her say of a novel, "It's too translucent." Of a painting, "Too choreographic." Of a poem, "Too thanatopsy." Now you take the ordinary proto-literate mentality and they are going to wonder *in what sense* a novel may be called translucent, a painting choreographic, and a poem thanatopsy. While the suckers who care are debating the sense of the adjective, the adverbial *too* is quivering in the back of the assaulted work.

Where the ear is tin to begin with and the predetermined intent is denial, how pointless for Johnny to spend his pre-doctoral years drudging through the Platonists, the Aristotelians, the Coleridgean, through Richards and Empson and Ransom and Chase, to prepare for systematic and high-sounding obfuscation when any punk with a swing-barreled "too" can as easily shoot out the light.

For prestige, for status, for a seat in the lifeboat while the great ship goes down, the swarming academic critics step on what they can and make nearly enough noise to overwhelm the signals they are supposed to relay. There is no one in sight to command them to shut up and start reading again. And if they are swept away with all they were supposed to cherish, it is not for their sake that I will be sorry to see them go.

Of what they had to tell us about literature, too much was too transmogrifying.

How Good Is a Good Book?

One of the classes I have taught for several years is devoted to the close examination of twentieth century short stories and novels. The procedure of the course—insofar as I can briefly summarize it—is to recognize and examine those separable achievements of the writer's imagination which altogether add up to the meaning and effect of the whole work.

The objective of the class is to show that a work of fiction represents the solution of a very considerable number of inter-related problems. For one thing, the writer must imagine his characters as individuals. Then he must imagine and demonstrate what all of them mean in the particular grouping or relationship in which he has cast them. He must show the changes in each and how these changes alter the relationships as he pushes his story along line by line and word by word. And . . . it isn't necessary to complete or even continue this list of concerns. They are well enough known to most of us.

Since such matters are among the tasks of a writer of fiction, it appears natural that the most valuable pleasure of the reader lies in recognizing, as he reads, each of the distinct solutions worked out by the author, those successful leaps of the imagination which are satisfying in themselves, though their principal contribution is to the satisfaction we get from the work as a whole.

And . . . I have found my students impatient of this approach. I am teaching them to read, they feel, when they already know how to read. Good. There ought to be a certain tension between teacher and students—resistance, tug-of-war, wrestling—or there would not be enough fun for any of us in the educational process. I hope always to accept this tension with gratitude, without impatience. And I think I could do so with a tranquil soul if I did not sense that each year my new bunch of students is a little more impatient than last year's group with such an approach. More impatient with the prolonged and complex involvements with a piece of literature which should be the chief reward of reading.

I don't mean that my students are lazy or lacking in intellectual capacity nor that in any circumstance they would admit, even to themselves, that they lack respect for literature. What scares me is the shadow of a pervading change, something half intangible in the atmosphere which goads and lures us all.

Many of my students are the cream of the crop. They are bright and sophisticated young men and women. Since most of them hope, however untested their hopes may be, to spend their lives as writers, they obviously dare not tolerate in their own minds the suspicion that fiction is losing its importance to them.

Yet it seems to me that impatience grows year by year. The new students will read. They will analyze—cleverly, too. But as they read they are impatient to be through with their labors so they can rest in possession of their nugget—their evaluation of the book as a whole, its place on some scale of rank. And I know they are cheated by their subtle conviction that this ultimate evaluation is what they really need. The nugget they hunt is not gold. They are doing very much what a man does who races through a splendid meal so he can enjoy the cigarette that settles his digestion at the end. Or what a man does when he makes love to a woman merely so he can tell himself or the gang at the corner that he has scored.

A few years ago in one of the earliest sessions of my class I read my students the following passage from Mark Twain's piece on Fenimore Cooper. Here Twain is talking about Cooper's novel *Deerslayer*. He is also, indirectly, talking about the opinion traders and taste makers who were happy to insist that, as a whole, *Deerslayer* is a Work of Art.

Twain groans: "A work of art? It has no invention; it has no order, system, sequence or result; it has no lifelikeness, no thrill, no stir, no seeming of reality; its characters are confusedly drawn, and by their acts and words they prove that they are not the sort of people the author claims they are; its humor is pathetic; its pathos is funny; its conversations are—oh! indescribable; its love scenes odious; its English a crime against the language.

"Counting these out, what is left is Art. I think we must all admit that."

Now, the satiric point of Twain's eruption is clear enough. When he puts his tongue in his cheek for those last two sentences, the cheek bulges like a chipmunk's trying to swallow a golf ball.

It seems to me a once-and-for-all rebuke to anyone who would dare ignore the component achievements or shortcomings in a piece of fiction and still have the gall to offer an evaluation —"good" or "bad," "a work of art"—of the work as a whole.

I read this passage to my class as an admonition *not* to race prematurely to evaluations; *not* to trust, ever, an evaluation that had not emerged straight from an addition of the elements that constituted the whole work—"the order, system, sequence . . . the seeming of reality . . . its conversations . . . its English." If I were teaching elementary arithmetic, I couldn't allow my students to solve problems in addition by drawing a horizontal line and writing an arbitrary number below it. The number below the line has to be the equivalent of all the numbers above it.

Now, of course we all know that whether an amateur reader or a professional critic makes an evaluation of a piece of fiction, he is not dealing with quantities as exact as those dealt with by mathematics. Nevertheless it seems to me, as it seemed to Twain, that any critic who does not follow a process analogous to that of adding a column of figures in coming to his final evaluation, is either a fool or a knave. He's stupid or he has a reason to lie.

I never meant to suggest to my class that they should or could dispense with evaluation in their reading. Would I ask someone to dinner and ask him not to taste what he ate? And if he tasted, he would inevitably enjoy some parts of the dinner more and some less. For his sake I would hope he didn't estimate the dinner good or bad merely by how much he enjoyed the cigarette at the end.

It seems to me that Goethe's prescription for critical procedure is still honorable and reliable, though it may lack the authority of a commandment from on high. He said the first thing to do is find out what the author has done. Second, determine if he has done it well. Third—third, *not* first—decide if it was worth doing. That seems to me to put evaluation in its proper place—where it is quarantined from the disadvantages of prejudgment.

At any rate, I had, in some sense, posted a warning to my class by reading them this bit from Twain. In conducting the class I leaned backward—more or less, it's hard to measure—to avoid giving evaluations of my own either to the parts or the whole of any of the novels we read that semester. I was particularly scrupulous not to intrude my evaluations of the parts or the whole of James Gould Cozzens' *By Love Possessed* because, as some of you may remember, this had been made into a controversial book by a partly subterranean campaign of attack set off by Dwight MacDonald's review in *Commentary*.

Now controversy may be a fine thing. Literary controversy may be among those "sane wars, sweet wars, lifegiving wars" that Whitman hoped would follow the insane carnage of the Civil War. It may also, depending on how it is waged, tend toward the destruction of those free processes of the mind and imagination that literature and literary discussion are supposed to enlarge. The appeal to slogans, to group solidarity, to the dubious loyalties of fear and loneliness may indeed accompany literary competition as it may accompany that hideous thing we have learned to call total war. Against these degenerative tendencies I think we ought to seek in books the means to independence, individual judgment, and all the mortal uncertainties that courage can sustain.

I had chosen to put *By Love Possessed* on the reading list because—to come no closer to an evaluation of it here—it seems to me a big book in several senses. There is a lot to talk about in it for people who are interested in the form or the content of modern American fiction. Does its complex manner represent and illumine the complex literary and popular sensibility of a crucial segment of America in our time? About this I felt we were in position to wage some fruitful controversy.

Only the angels who keep the golden record are certain whether our classroom controversy was fruitful rather than obscurantist. At any rate, in the class and around it we had controversy, and, at the moment it seemed concluded, I could still hope that individually the students were going to value the book—negatively or positively—according to what they had found in it of order, system, lifelikeness, language, and so on. Then, a few weeks after the semester ended one of my very best students—a young poet for whom I have the highest hopes and the highest respect—was talking to me privately about the class and the way it had been conducted. He mentioned our wrangles over *By Love Possessed* and said, "You know, I think the class would have felt easier if you'd indicated from the beginning whether you thought it was a good book or not."

My chin went down like shoes. I couldn't believe that this young man of all the class hadn't understood what Twain meant when he threw his hammer at the fools and frauds who want to ignore the working parts of a novel when they decide whether or not to call it a work of art. But still he wished I had said, with no demonstration to support my feeling, that I had thought it was good or bad, a piece of wastepaper or a work of art that transcended or made negligible all questions of its political, social, domestic, psychological, logodaedalic truth. Then the partisan opponents of the book would have known throughout the discussion what sort of fellow they had to deal with in me. The wide-eyed note takers could have felt secure that they were not wasting more attention and penmanship than the book deserved. That they were, or were not, missing a good bet. But a teacher is not a bookie.

As I say, I can't believe that this bright young man was insensible of Twain's warning. I'm afraid that what I do believe is that he heard certain evil whispers in the air of our times that sounded more imperative to him. Whispers that asked, "How are you on the goose?"

Back in the days when the territory of Kansas was disputed —whether it would go slave or go free—men asked each other when they met, "How are you on the goose?" Which meant, which side are you on? And then they shot it out or buddied up, depending on the answer. "I'm agin it." Or "I'm for it." I have never been able to free myself of the thought that the men of either party who consented to participate in such over-simplified dialogue were voting "slave" whether their sympathies were Northern or Southern.

Yet I believe that such partisan simplification is far more justified in politics than it could be in literary activities. The thought weighs very heavily on me that those who are satisfied to hear if a book be good or bad are opting for slavery, for their own stupefaction in that area where the costs of freedom are least and its rewards greatest, in the area of the mind.

If there is a progress, an entropic drift toward that condition in which no one will ask more about a book than whether it is a "good book" or not, of course the responsibilities for this drift are divided. Some share of it goes to those passive sheep who feel the blessings of togetherness if they agree with their peer group on what is good. Some share of it goes to those manipulators of the national taste, high and low, whose power, great or small, depends on being dictators of the arts.

However it comes about, by drift, by greed, as a by-product of the anxieties we all share about the fate of the race in these unprecedented times, the reduction of judgments about books to good or bad—ours or theirs—is a fascist business, the despair of democracy. It reduces—on private levels, among students, among people to whom books are almost the blood of life—it reduces talk about books to the obscene and infantile level of trading "my good book" for "your good book" like children exchanging TV trading cards.

Among the people I have chiefly associated with in the last several years it would seem particularly unsophisticated to say, "I cried when Little Nell died," or "if I could have got ahold of that Percy Grimm I'd have stomped him to death," or "I really knew how Lucy Honeychurch felt when she said to old Mr. Webster, 'Kiss me and I will try.' "

I guess comments of that sort should sound quaint. They are like the behavior of the yokel at the theater who leans over the balcony railing to warn the heroine against the machinations of the villain.

But, oh my dears, how much better such talk is than a dialogue that goes like this:

"How's Baldwin's new book?"

"It's not as good as *The Assistant.* I liked it better than *The Invisible Man.* It's not as good as his essays."

That is the dialogue of those who have been to our classes in criticism, who have been to the big town and seen how the game is played, who consent to the imposition of a kind of star system on literature. I hear it all the time. Poor devils. The yokel readers have it all over them.

I do not see how in the teaching of literature—any more than in its publication, the compilation of anthologies, the advertisement and reviewing of new works—we can get away from authority and prejudice. Without authority and prejudice there would be a hopeless disorder in a student's encounter with literature, in the encounter of the reading public with the books available in their time.

A teacher, like a reviewer or an editor, must assume the responsibility of saying, either flatly or in effect, "This is worth your reading, and that is not, or is less worth reading, or should not be read until you have read something else." But there are various objectives to be sought in the process of selection and guidance in reading, some tending to make a place for literature in the social and intellectual life of our time, others spoiling literature for largely undeclared social, intellectual, or commercial advantages. It seems to me that any educational or distributive machinery which tends to reduce judgment about books to labels of good or bad is an abuse of authority and prejudice.

We are all conditioned to agree that books are a blessing. They can be misused like those other blessings, fire and alcohol. We've all known misreaders—ourselves if no one else—who've opened good books and slothfully read into their pages what we expected to find rather than what is actually there. Readers who turn the pages of *Anna Karenina* and mentally ingest the sequel to *Marjorie Morningstar*. Readers who find that Shylock is the hero of *The Merchant of Venice*. (If we have no more subtle ways of discriminating the evils of anti-Semitism than by composing a list of good guys who *weren't* anti-Semitic, Shakespeare of course included, and bad guys who were and reading everything in the smoky lamplight of this prejudice, then we have no rational defense against racism. It seems to breed in one kind of stagnant mental swamp as well as in another.) In times of war like the present we can read occasionally objective accounts of courage or of inhumanity and convert our interpretations of courageous or bestial acts into their opposite according to which flag covers them. In fact, we are expected to make these conversions automatically, and those experienced in handling public opinion have every reason to be confident of their expectations in such matters.

So we know that what we call books in the broadest sense— the testimonies of the printed page—can be converted into one sort of testimony or another by the kind of reading they are given. If we cling to the idea that some books are inherently good, others less so, we are still hardly at liberty to ignore the career of that book—when it is read, how it is read, and by whom. We are admonished by Scripture to consider the merit of words spoken *in due season*. Spoken when they will count— not when their appropriateness has become negligible or of merely formal interest. Every reader conscious of his own mental history knows that he has encountered some books out of season—when he is not prepared for them or when they no longer pertain to his most vital interests. What he finds in his own life must surely be multiplied infinitely in a populous world of many books. Which should make him very cautious of the proposition that the value of books can be stably fixed.

Books are things, and good things can be bad. A book in which order, system, sequence, and result are present with their offer of sweetness and light can, in the misuse of its authority and good name, be the instrument of obscurantism.

Therefore I have raised the somewhat silly sounding question, how good is a good book? How good was that good book you were curled up with last night? I think those of us whose business is books and ideas are, in a petrifying time, under the heaviest of obligations to resist the comfort of clichés, of vested academic or publishing interests, and keep this absurd, all-important question open. We have a continuing obligation to state it and its implications as clearly as we can to those we profess to teach.

To begin with we should make clear that the question branches in two ways—or draws from two component ideas of value. One: What is a book good *for?* Two: What *inherent* value has it? In our critical processes we are obliged to keep these components in some degree distinct, but never to let them get entirely separated.

And though we have to forego quick or comforting statements of position, we should be constantly willing to deal with the riddling variations we will get when we try to evaluate one single work with these component approaches.

For example, suppose I ask for an off-the-cuff evaluation of *The Faerie Queene, The Sun Also Rises,* and a novel by Horatio Alger. Each of these books proposes to teach a code by which men ought to conduct themselves. Now if we ask what these books have been good for, I suppose we'll tend to agree that each of them may indeed have helped individuals, many or few, conduct themselves better than they would have if they had not read the books. Then . . . were the individuals helped by the Alger novel less valuable to society or in the eye of God than those directed by *The Faerie Queene?* We are forbidden to think so, and we also understand that a book which might be nearly worthless for a mature mind could, by fortunate coincidence, cause some well nigh magical transformation in a reader not yet mature. My friend the painter Byron Burford is always recalling to me the pulp magazines and adventure books which enchanted and fixed his imagination many years ago, and in his paintings now we can see some impressive sign of what those books were good for. And we recall Joyce's predilection for magpie reading all his life. Reading the back of a cereal box is good for the imagination of a genius.

Even so, we would feel a very proper reluctance to admitting that *The Faerie Queene, The Sun Also Rises,* and the Alger novel were equally good even if, somehow, it could be shown that the reading of the three had produced equally beneficent results.

Most of us, paying a tribute to academic pieties, would say that *The Faerie Queene* was *inherently* better than the other two examples. From our own reading experience and those habits of aesthetic and intellectual appreciation that have been trained into us we would remain assured that *The Sun Also Rises* is inherently better than the Alger novel. Whether Hemingway's code has helped us live better lives or not, there are images of ourselves and our state in Hemingway that we would hardly give up just for the sake of being happy or good. And if we found, as most of us undoubtedly would, that we appreciated *The Sun Also Rises* more than we appreciated *The Faerie Queene,* our irrational loyalty to tradition could still be rationally justified by the hypothesis that an ideal reader would respond to the order, system, and sequence of *The Faerie Queene* as we, creatures of our time, can not. If a Joyce found, as he might—as he might—that the inherent superiority lay in the Alger novel, we would try as hard as we could to accommodate this apparent breach of order by supposing that he was making imaginative additions to the Alger text—that, analogous to the slothful reader who converts *Anna Karenina* to *Marjorie Morningstar,* Joyce was reading *Finnegan's Wake* while he turned the pages of *Poor But Honest.*

For without faith in those aspects of intellect and the emotional life which have no perceptible results in conduct, the whole establishment of literature would quickly collapse. If the value of books were ever located exclusively in what they are good for, then all authority in literary evaluation should be instantly surrendered to the behavioral sciences.

The position to which we defenders of the literary experience are willy-nilly committed is not one of stasis, or final, rock-bottom stability, but of perpetual equilibrium. We've got to keep one foot riding the values that are measurable by their consequences, the other on those values we have been taught to prize for themselves. We dare not ever repudiate Maugham's *Of Human Bondage,* because we know that at one stage of a young man's journey it can, it does, it should stand like a lighthouse. Books of this order, remembered for what they once may have done, continue to show a reader where he has been as they once showed him where he had to go. In the name of balance we must sustain a respect for seldom-read books like *The Faerie Queene* or *Finnegan's Wake,* though their treasures are nearly as inaccessible to us as gold mines on Mars, and for most of us little use even as pastimes or puzzles.

We live in a world of onrushing time and no one forgets that except at his peril. We dare not linger too long in the chambers of the sea nor on the drill field of the practical. While we linger, the profiteers are turning "inherent values" to their personal advantage by selling a low-brow generation a million shelves full of high-brow books. The sloganeers peddle, under vulgar aesthetic slogans, the books that might have taught us to live more justly. The subject matter of social protest is becoming, by a process of creeping Algrenism (named in honor of Nelson Algren), a taste divorced from the social purpose that justified it a few decades ago. MacDonaldism (named in honor of Dwight MacDonald) makes high-brow snobbery available at modest prices, and readers who are not really up to reading Edna St. Vincent Millay are stocking their shelves with Mallarmé and Valery. Mailerism (named in honor of Norman Mailer) honors the principle of condensation by suggesting that writers are in competition, like heavyweight prizefighters. They are competing to produce just one novel—which Mr. Mailer likes to call The Bitch. The implication is that once The Bitch has been achieved, then no reader, critic, or writer eliminated from the competition need bother about lesser novels, and, by extension, need not *read* The Bitch but merely concede it is The Best. *Best* as a label is the superlative trading card for the stupefied minds now carrying on the empty dialogue of "what books are good."

I anticipate that moment when The Bitch is enshrined as the moment when Henry Adams' heat death will be accomplished, when those familiar motions of the spirit that we have recognized as literary will all cease.

And there are so many powers and principalities progressing toward that moment that I do not know if they can be halted. I have no overall program of national reform to propose—not even a clear notion of what I should propose to do in my own small corner of the academic and book reviewing world. In supposing that such comment as *this* might be good for something I merely permit myself to hope that I can define a stance by which those of us who choose to may feel most freely at home in the unglaciated areas left to us here and now.

In that spirit I want to propose my notions of what a book is best *for* and what is *inherently* best in a book.

Primarily a book is good *for* leading us on to other books. A novel by Horatio Alger is doing its best when it leads the individual or many individuals on to consider the more complex and illuminated views of conduct in *The Sun Also Rises* and *The Faerie Queene.*

A book is inherently good if it declares some part of the truth of human experience not declared in other books. Its inherent goodness is most easily accessible if we take it to be part of a vast dialogue—hardly accessible at all if we see it as one among many competitors for a single crown.

I don't believe in good books at all except as a consequence of believing in the goodness and necessity of literature. A novel —any novel you might choose to value—is good because fiction is good, because fiction nourishes and extends many lives and experiences beyond our own present. A poem is good because poetry is good. It can not be the other way around. If this sounds like a tricky or precarious thought, let me claim that I am merely making an analogy from our common ways of appreciating goodness in human beings. Our belief, for instance, that Abraham Lincoln is a good man, must come—can only come—as a consequence of believing in the goodness of humanity. It can not come from believing he was better than a pack of rats whom he somehow mistakenly loved and rose above.

To believe in a pluralistic republic of books has this overwhelming advantage over believing in the messianic Bitch that will someday make democratic untidiness and diversity unnecessary: It permits one to expect wisdom, sweetness, and light in the relationship between two or more books as well as within their individual covers. Lawrence's *Lady Chatterley's Lover* makes an impressive statement about adultery and the rights and liberty of the individual. Tolstoy's *Anna Karenina* makes an impressive statement about adultery and the rights and liberty of the individual. The statements do not agree. How shall we reconcile them?

One way is to decide which is the best of the two novels, put the best one on the throne and behead the other. There are too many books, aren't there? The glut in any library makes the glut of surplus corn in our country look like the savings of normal thrift. Why not get rid of the inferior junk?

The other way to reconcile books that disagree is to recognize that their statements, ideological or esthetic, so final-seeming within the pasteboard covers of a single work, are a part of a continuing dialogue in the pluralistic worlds of fiction, poetry, drama, or whatever.

It is the multiplicity in fiction and poetry, the discords, contradictions, harmonies, extensions, intransigent qualifications, and the brute hoarding of experience that makes the habitable world of literature. All this is "life enhancing," to use Berenson's great phrase. This multiplicity gives resonance and hope to our practical lives, makes the great difference between the despair of the human condition and the confidence of the human spirit.

As a sort of postscript, let me briefly suggest the implications of my position for programs of literary studies, particularly the study of contemporary literature. I am not talking about curriculum. Curriculum is as curriculum does and we all know that a school with a beautifully balanced offering of courses, a catalogue that might be an aesthetic joy forever, may or may not be the perfect place for the study of literature.

I guess I am concerned with an attitude toward the subject and with a pretense that I consider as obstructive as it is prevalent. The pretense is that by assigning and explicating "the best" of twentieth century literature we have given the student the keys to understanding the meanings of literature in his own time. I think this is merely a convenient pretense, and is responsible sometimes for putting the academies in positions of being unpaid salesmen for publishing houses that have vested, unexamined interests in certain reputations and titles. I hope I have at least begun to suggest some of the permanent difficulties in determining what is the best.

Why not assign and explicate, in our courses in modern literature, "the worst"? If what we call, with a certain amount of unjustifiable facility, the worst of contemporary literature were well understood, I think this understanding might open many new perspectives on the best.

For one thing, we ought to remember and heed Valery's comment in his book on Leonardo that "the working of the mind of an idiot is more interesting than the productions of genius." Do you understand that? It means that Nature, working through all the manifestations of its human agency, is the great and everlasting subject of our quest for knowledge and quest for beauty. That reading, properly defined, means a comprehension, greater or lesser, of the nature of literary phenomena, not the "mastery of a field" or a discipline, which is always to a large extent rote learning.

Why not study the idiotic as well as the expression of genius in contemporary literature? Those who have done so have looked from peaks of Darien that are simply unguessed by a great many professional critics of modern letters.

The French say slyly, *Le vrai est le secret de quelqu'un.* Meaning, the truth is somebody's secret. The aim of any study, including literary study, is to make it possible for anybody to know what somebody knows. And in this matter of the relation between the idiotic and the sublime in contemporary letters, I am well convinced that some people know more than others about the kinships.

Let me not labor the idea that the worst ought to be purposely included, but let me pass on to a brief statement of why the good, staple current of things that might be casually labeled second rate are not only a valuable, but perhaps invaluable part of a course of study in contemporary literature. I think that all literary teaching worthy of the name is a matter of comparisons—and not gross comparisons of theme and attitude toward life but minute and detailed comparisons of structure, language, pattern, and so on. I have found it easier to make these comparisons, which have everything to do with the understanding of art as art, by moving freely between the great names and the unrecognized ones. Tolstoy's story *The Death of Ivan Ilyich* seems to me a very hard story to talk about critically—and perhaps the most important thing to say about it is just that nothing needs to be said about it. To give the proper inflection to this silence, it is important to show that explication can unfold the art and meaning of, say, a story by Jean Stafford, H. L. Davis, Richard Yates, or J. D. Salinger. I have a feeling that a course that contained only works by Tolstoy, James, Lawrence, Kafka, and Faulkner would not, perhaps, teach students as much about the art of Tolstoy, James, Lawrence, Kafka, and Faulkner as one which was interspersed with the works of other less famous writers.

It seems to me that the attitude of the teacher of contemporary literature ought to be that in preparing a reading list— whether for a course or a whole program of study—he is bringing together those works which will on the one hand serve as standards of excellence (when we talk about standards, remember that the centimeter is as important to the system of measurement as the mile) and on the other sensitize the developing students to the complexities, variations, and practices of the literary art in our time. The aim is not to put them in possession of treasures that they can guard zealously for the rest of their lives, but to prepare them to take nourishment from and pass effective judgments on the diverse reading matter that will confront them hereafter.

The Sears and Ward
Catalogues: 1964

SEARS CATALOGUE: Spring and Summer, 1964. Illustrated. Sears, Roebuck. 1,715 pp. Free.

WARDS CATALOGUE: Spring and Summer, 1964. Illustrated. Montgomery Ward. 1,340 pp. Free.

Wayward as my own uses of them may be, I would never doubt that Sears and Ward publish these more than Bible-sized books—totaling 3,055 pages between them this spring—to sell goods. I am sure this primary intent of theirs is achieved with superb efficiency. I know that I've been drawing from their cornucopia of material blessings since my folks bought me a mail-order violin for my fifth Christmas. In this past year I've ordered through the catalogues a mattress, a set of tires, a Chemcraft set, two Superman suits complete with scarlet capes, and a nurse's uniform for a four-year-old girl. We're doing business, Sears, Ward, and I.

But aside from that, all these years I've been one among uncounted citizens who read the Sears and Ward pages for gratifications of a literary or para-literary order. We read for images of ourselves, of the constancy rather than the crises of our collective lives, and for analyses of the logistics of happiness.

Tolstoy said that all happy families are alike—thereby repudiating them as fit subjects for fiction and leaving them without a literary *genre* they can call their own, unless as I aver, these catalogues firmly and modestly declare not only their eixstence but its qualities.

In Wallace Stegner's story, "Bugle Song," there is a passage to illustrate how a devoted reader feels incorporated into the story told by Sears and Ward:

> ". . . days when the baked clay of the farmyard cracked in the heat and the sun brought cedar smells from fence posts . . . he lay dreaming on the bed in the sleeping porch with a Sears Roebuck catalogue open before him, picking out the presents he would buy for his mother and his father and his friends next Christmas. . . ."

It's clear the boy is doing more than picking out presents. He is picking out new mothers and fathers and friends, too. (There's Mom in her BOUCLE KNIT of Orlon Acrylic and Nylon, The Middy Look, stepping across a green lawn of a kindlier corner of the Republic; there's Dad out in the big woods cutting lodging costs with a Ted Williams Camper-Trailer, $488., No Money Down; and the real pals, friendly, vital lads and lasses, are with him in a Corru-Ribbed Steel Wall Swimming Pool, $32.88, beach ball not included—buy ladder separately.) Neither Fenimore Cooper nor Edgar Rice Burroughs will ever give him a place in their stories as cozy, familiar, and easy as this.

But identification, however jolly, is a primitive sort of literary experience, and I have in mind something beyond that. Along with Stegner's picture of an apprentice reader, I'd set up the figure of a more mature fellow, lounging at midnight in his book-lined study, not so much jaded by his wide critical surveys of modern literature as *prepared* to leap over the *genre* wall and look in the catalogues with wild surmise at "meanings unknown before"—at a form that dares essay the unsung multiplicity of democratic experience.

This older reader knows, from Joseph Frank's *Spatial Form in Modern Literature,* that in Eliot, Pound, and Proust "the reader is intended to apprehend their work spatially, in a moment of time, rather than as a sequence." So he's not going to plunge into the catalogues expecting to find stories told in old-fashioned narrative sequence. To get the Poundian, Eliotic effect of simultaneity, one's got to note the montage—which,

for an example from Ward's, puts the "AIRLINE ACOUSTI-
CAL GUITARS, Suitable For Solo or Orchestra" on the page
following the Union Suits ("Extra Comfort! Brent Year 'Round
Weights"). It's the juxtaposition of such pages that "presents
an intellectual and emotional complex in an instant of time"—
like, just turn the page rapidly and see *who* is wearing his Brent
Union Suit on an August night while he plays his "Best Arch
Top Mastersize Cutaway Airline Acoustical Guitar" at the
VFW dance. What other prose or verse could body forth that
strummer with such speed and vividness?

My hypothetical reader is, of course, familiar with O'Hara's
device of particularizing a character by his clothing labels,
which become in turn an index of his campus affiliations. Adopt-
ing that procedure our man need turn only a few catalogue
pages to evoke a legion of young men stepping across the
campuses of DeKalb U., Platteville S. T. C., or Pikeville J. C.,
not one of them anonymous in his Arvalon slacks, Brent shirt,
Oakbrook jacket, and PowrHouse shoes. And the girls who
wait for them—each a vibrant individual in her Carol Brent
pumps, Brentshire cocktail dress, and Sally Victor hat. Far from
the capitols of fiction, there are very many more of them than
there are young men wearing J. Press suits to meetings of Skull
and Bones.

Nathanael West has prepared our reader to look sharp for
alienated souls, and Sears isn't really determined to keep them
out of sight in the happiness picture. On page 871 they adver-
tise "Weights-You-Wear." There's nothing superficially odd,
I suppose, about a vest that holds "ten to twenty pounds remov-
able lead weights" since this weights idea "figures big in Air
Force jet pilot training." But . . . "you can even wear these
weights under dress clothes. . . ." (Oh, Miss Lonelyhearts, I
was dancing with this fellow at the Hunt Ball and something
kept bumping. . . .)

Lost, pleading eyes peer through the shrubbery of announce-
ments like: "Sizes for Shorter Women, Women, and Tall
Women." (I loved him, Miss Lonelyhearts, but he preferred
a Woman.) Or in Sears roundabout justification for custom
tailoring: "Whether you're 7 ft. 3 in. or 3 ft. 7 in. tall . . .

whether your waist is 16 in. or 61 in. Sears can fit you correctly."
(Miss Lonelyhearts, I am 3 ft. 7 in. tall and have a 61 in.
waist, and though my suit from Sears fits me "as perfectly as
it does the gentleman on the right" of their ad, I do not look
like the gentleman at the right, who looks like one of the
Rockefellers.)

On the whole, though—and we must never forget how
numerous and vast a whole it is—the catalogues triumphantly
maintain that within the facile measures of charlatans crying
"Conformity!" and existentialists refusing the patent of "Essence" to the common continuum of happiness there is yet an
almost infinite variety of valuable human patterns.

In these confident pages the accumulation of imperatives—
"Enjoy . . .! Dress Up . . .! Save . . .! Protect . . .! Exercise
daily, the easy way . . .!"—becomes an atmosphere of motherly
admonition, permissive but determined that all our happy ones
shall be comely, decent, *and* abreast of the times. On page 18
Sears advertises "The Bikini to Change Your Mind." The
lightly hidden meaning of this slogan is clarified by the illustration of the garment in question. It's a bikini, all right, I guess,
but it's offered in a ginghamy check of decent black and white,
cut modestly enough to overcome a girl's scruples against bikini
exposure. Its superb highlight of compromise is a waistband
that covers exactly one half of the model's navel. "What's
intriguing is the misty-dark cover of a jacket." Shipping weight,
1 pound.

In the ladies' pages most of the color photography is indistinguishable from that in slick women's magazines except for
the absence of the haunting, pederastic glimmer we have been
taught to recognize as the true hallmark of fashion photography.

There is very little in the catalogues that could properly be
called luxury goods. Though Sears' first offering is a 3-carat
diamond priced at $6,500, though wigs are available (100%
European Hair, $119.95) and "Original Works of Fine Art"
(mail this coupon to Dept. 9921 for Graphics Catalog), the
condition of American happiness seems to consist less in the
anticipation of luxury than in the assurance that no seemly
hungers will be denied. Almost every kind of item on offer is

backed up in depth—there are reasonable facsimiles of "Our Best" at lower and then at rock-bottom prices. Behind the ready-to-wear sits the sewing machine.

In the women's clothing section the anxiety not to be exclusive carries the cataloguers to the point of offering mastectomy bras to "restore natural figure balance" for ladies bereft of bosoms. Just as there are many pages where infants in HONEYSUCKLE garb beam from their "New! Expanding" playpens, there are symmetric pages of wheel chairs, hearing aids, and hospital beds for happy elders. Pad-O-Matic is a " 'must' for the bed-ridden person: 20 air tubes alternately and silently inflate and deflate, providing gentle, constantly changing support." The American Ivan Ilyches will never get into Tolstoyan novels of unhappy family life. I see them rather riding in their Patient Lifters ($199 . . . "allows smooth, comfortable transfer from bed to wheel chair, wheel chair to auto") and getting all the spiritual consolation they require from "family Bibles that give you so much . . . maps . . . full concordance . . . beautiful illustrations."

For the reader of judgment, the catalogues provide perspective on the much-maligned spirit of "do-it-yourself." What both books affirm—to take a minimal example—is that there are in this nation people who will buy a 45-cent wheel cylinder repair kit to rebuild a wheel cylinder that costs only $2.45 brand new. (Have you ever wrestled off a worn and rusted wheel cylinder, let alone rebuilding and replacing it? Tremble, oh, you push-button tyrants.) They affirm that on the ranches and farms and in backyards and if need be on the public domain or the railroads' rights-of-way there will be descendants of the old self-reliant breed to take in hand a set of four brake shoes ($3.69 *with trade-in*) and with a borrowed kit of hub-pullers, spring pliers, and lock-ring pliers restore the brakes of anything back to a '46 De Soto, or a '40 Buick, or perhaps even a '27 Stutz.

Oh, they're still out there. They may be easing back with their "fish Lo-K-Tors" (which work "on the sonar principle" to reveal how many fish are under the boat), but Sears and

Ward prophesy that they're ready as ever to make a comely new world.

And yet one sees them—in reverse image on the catalogue pages — as uncertain where they should be most confident, shaken by intimations of what the Ben Franklin policy of uprightness won't cover, so they have to be redundantly assured. The cataloguers, who seem to know, picture these people as needing two justifications for a thing where one should do. "Decorative as well as functional." "Beautiful as well as durable." (Don't they know, "the body dies, the body's beauty lives"?) "Convenient as well as stylish."

Way over on page 1,360 Sears advertises a POPULAR CAST-IRON CANNON HEATER. "An old-time favorite. Non-burning, use it as a planter, divider, or 'conversation-piece.'" That's the kind of redundant dubiety that troubles me. I would like to rise from reading the catalogues with the conviction that the heater will never be used as mere "conversation-piece." I want to come to the end believing it will be bought by a Wright Morris character out in Lone Tree, Nebraska. That he will put some corncobs in it, light it, and put his feet up on it. And feel he doesn't need to say a word—just wait quietly.

Tarzan Lives

When the psychiatry of our time finishes listing its categories of disorder, among them will surely be the tarzanal (or tarzanoid) personality. In popular jargon the condition may be called tarzanity. Most of us lay diagnosticians have long since recognized the classic manifestations of the tarzanic syndrome. We have seen its outbreak in gymnasia, public parks, boys' dormitories, and at swimming pools. Wherever spindly youth, pot-bellied middle age, and even muscular beef in the prime can find a horizontal bar to dangle from, it will betimes emit the throat-stretching warble of Lord Greystoke, Tarzan of the Apes.

Hybrid of joke and devotion, mixture of sheer exhibitionism with mythic role playing, conglomerate of self-mockery and demonic possession, the impulse to make like Tarzan has or will have at one time affected the lives of most American males. It has been estimated that one tenth of our male population is, at any given time, tarzanoid.

The iconic Tarzan figure that thus usurps the place of our egos was, of course, the invention of a pulp writer who became one of the most popular authors of our century. Between the publication of *Tarzan of the Apes* in 1914 and his death in 1950, Edgar Rice Burroughs became as wealthy and famous as he was prolific. As author of the Tarzan books and many science fiction adventures, he rose from the status of unsuccessful businessman to become a one-man corporation. He lived in a town that had, in a manner of speaking, issued directly from his literary imagination—Tarzana, California.

Beyond this, however, Burroughs enjoyed the distinction of incorporating as part of his subject matter the effect that his hero had upon the psyche of his readers. Though Sophocles is honored as the delineator of Oedipus, there is no extant play in which Oedipus tangles with a victim of the Oedipus complex. But in *Tarzan and the Madman* (published now, posthumously, for the first time) the true Tarzan is embroiled with a tarzanal personality—one of those uncounted Americans *who thinks he is Tarzan!* On his own turf, Tarzan is aped.

Colin T. Randolph, Jr. of West Virginia may be generically labeled a "madman" in the title of this lost work of the master. But there is no doubt in the mind of the other characters as to the precise nature of the pathology displayed.

" 'What did the imposter call himself?' asked the Englishman.

" 'Tarzan of the Apes.'

"Bolton-Chilton scratched his head. 'It must be contagious,' he said."

Right you are, brave Bolton-Chilton! Elsewhere in the novel we are told how Colin T. caught the bug. The process of infection may be considered standard. He "used to talk a lot about Tarzan of the Apes." (Like Carl H. Paul, Jr., Johnny Rogers, and me the summer after we saw the Weismuller Tarzan film in Nebraska City, Neb.) "He said he had read so much about him for years and had admired him so much that he decided to emulate him." (Off the stepladder we leaped for the jerking bagswing, yodeling like hairless apes.) "He practiced at archery until he was pretty good with a bow-and-arrow." (Carl and I used to knock the beans off the catalpa tree in his grandmother's yard with arrow after arrow.)

Unlike Carl and Johnny and you and me, Colin gets a buddy to fly him to the heart of Africa. He goes for a bet of 1,000 pounds sterling which will be his if he can subsist like Tarzan for a month in the jungle. When he parachutes from the crippled plane, a little teeny bump on the head extinguishes the last flicker of sense that enabled him to distinguish himself from the true King of the Apes. Hereafter, to the confusion of the Dark Continent, its natives, its exploiters, and one Sandra Pickerall, a wealthy, beautiful, and instinctively virtuous English girl, there are two Tarzans at large grappling with the African fauna.

Aping the Ape Man, Colin almost instantly infringes the code of his idol—perhaps because he lacks Greystoke blood to keep him true. Burroughs set much store by good blood. Persuaded by a lost civilization of degenerate Portuguese that he is God, Colin becomes the supplier of native women for their obscene Portagee blood orgies and presently abducts Sandra Pickerall herself. He leads her through cannibal country at the end of a leash, up an escarpment and into the lost kingdom, where she is to be his goddess.

Little good that rank will do Sandra, for the King and his High Priest have only proclaimed the divinity of Colin in order to fool the people. With an English girl in their clutches they show their true colors. The King sneaks into her apartment first and impertinently asks her name.

" 'My name is Sandra,' she replied: 'but you may call me either Holy One or Goddess. Only the gods may call me Sandra.'

" 'Come, come,' he said. 'Let's be friends. Let's not stand on ceremony. After all, I am a king. You may call me Chris if you wish to.' "

Not Sandra. She cools him in the English manner. But the High Priest, of Semitic mien, "definitely hawklike," is a tougher customer. After "her slaves prepared her for bed," he gets into her apartment and is dragging her "to the couch" when the American Tarzan-faker appears to kick him out. Colin may be lacking a few marbles, but he knows what you can and can't do to the daughter of a wealthy Englishman. After all, Colin "had her in his power for a long time and he had never offered her even the slightest incivility."

In the meantime (alternate chapters) the true, the singular, the legitimate Tarzan is swinging through the trees in pursuit of the nut who is ruining his reputation. Respectful only of the higher law (known best to the higher apes; sullied by human equivocations), Tarzan intends to kill the wretch as soon as he gets within bow shot.

For the author to put his multitude of characters in non-concentric African orbits makes for a lightning pace and an incredible series of complications. But neither of these qualities explains the appeal that this, like the earlier Tarzan books, has for the tarzanally predisposed perpetual pre-pubescent. I locate this appeal in three tried and true Burroughs elements: (1) ineptitude of style, (2) polymorphous, watered down, elegantly camouflaged sexuality, and (3) the essentially static, invulnerable, and omnipotent figure of the Ape Man, a usably vulgarized incarnation of the Archetype of the Child (cf. Jung).

The style—sentence by sentence and scene by scene—appeals to the marginally literate reader as being the way he might express himself if he were writing the book. He is as at home with the gaudy little ornaments and archaisms as with the sterility of the plain statements. The attempts to hammer square pegs of language into the round holes of concept are, in themselves, signals at once reassuring and evocative. Consider: "Presently Kyomya came with raiment; and it was raiment, not just ordinary clothing or even apparel." (How would you kids like to see your fifth-grade teacher strutting around in some *raiment?* How about that, huh?)

Second—the nudity of Tarzan is insistently played upon. In earlier books his sole garb was called a loin cloth. In this offering to an evolved popular sensibility, he is "naked but for a G-string." " '. . . . a great big guy comes into camp wearing nothing but a G-string.' " Now a G-string, as E.R.B. and all his readers know, has no anthropological or outdoor connotations whatsoever. It is irremediably associated with the erotic display of the human body. The trick accomplished here is to combine mild, androgynous eroticism with a context that affirms it's all just natural under the circumstances. Beauty-and-the-Beast combinations—as of Sandra Pickerall and the "great apes" who fight over her—are hinted in a language so vapid that it serves as a kind of stylistic "plain wrapper" for the lurid possibilities implied.

Most important of all in the Burroughs mix is the imperturbable image, unchanging as a figure on a Grecian urn, of the hero. ". . . by gad, he inspires confidence. Somehow I feel safe when he's around. . . ." So says Bolton-Chilton. So say we all. It is pointless to examine the quality or interest of Tarzan's adventures. At best or at worst they are mere excuses to give us a glimpse of that big, naked nightingale amid the leaves. Far from the fever and the fret of the normal world, he swings through the forest glade of our urban day dreams. Singing—for that is really what he is doing when he gives the victory cry of the bull ape—he will always sing the confidence and uncertainty of a boy's hesitation at the threshold of manhood. The madness of emulation he has inspired in us all is, however vain and vulgar, an expression of our discontent with mechanization. Lacking better gods, we owe him the tribute of occasional tarzanity.

Accusers and Pardoners

"Radix malorum est cupiditas," said the Pardoner who rode with the Canterbury Pilgrims.

"The root of evil is conformity," say many popular books of the last decade—*White Collar, The Lonely Crowd, The Status Seekers,* and several others with titles that stick in the mind like slogans.

Surely both these precepts are dandy and familiar, their origins impeccable, and their favorable reception guaranteed. Before Emerson said it, others were telling Americans to be self-reliant. We're still grateful for any help we can get in living up to this ideal.

Nevertheless we recall that a purpose lurked and twisted under the moral covering of the story told by Chaucer's Pardoner. A second look at his tale showed him to be a prime apologist for the Prince of Darkness. Other examples, even some drawn from our secular democracy, could show that a tyranny over the mind has no better allies than those who sell easy answers to hard questions. So a second look at the new books that bid us flee conformity may be in order, just to make sure that their purpose is as good as their moral.

Suppose a voice, not exactly from heaven but from a respectable elevation, were to charge us, "You have sinned against passion and truth . . . against Eros and Pallas Athena, and not by any heavenly intervention, but by the ordinary course of nature those allied deities will be avenged." We know there are secular Pardoners on hand, false critics, who would prompt us to answer, "I admit I've been doing a little togetherness on the sly. I conformed!" Or to confess, "I was a Mom!" But whoever told us we could cop a plea with the watchful gods, or with the ordinary course of nature, for that matter?

Suppose some foreigner (denied "intellectual responsibility" by the *Partisan Review* troop, but still able to watch from a vantage point) should remind us, "President Eisenhower has counted in tens of millions the innocent victims of the Rosenbergs; each of you feels already dead in some future war; these are the deaths which demanded death . . . for the ones who stole the atomic secret.

"Unhappily, when seen from Europe, you do not appear to be either innocent or dead. . . ."

If, after many years, that pricks conscience too painfully, we can always agree with Norman Mailer that "the Rosenberg case was boring."

Why not cop a plea? If we doubt that the gods exist, why shouldn't we doubt that the ordinary course of nature exists or ought to excite our interest?

I have no wish to categorize a group of writers that includes C. Wright Mills, David Riesman, Alan Harrington, A. C. Spectorsky, William H. Whyte, Jr., and Vance Packard as all being secular Pardoners. Some of them do considerably better service than peddling as relics the thighbone of a great idea or pieces of the veil worn by the Founding Fathers.

I would only like to suggest that all these authors (except perhaps Mills) represent a "style of thinking," to use Karl Mannheim's phrase; and, by making some observations on that style, raise the question of whether these books are really intended to heal us.

A style of thinking is partly definable by its exclusions, by the mere citation of ideas which are, within its limits, unthinkable. And we must remember, first of all, that these books come to us in the maturity of a social process in which ideas have been treated as commodities—and where, as a consequence, that which becomes unsaleable becomes presently unthinkable.

Take an idea from a moralist on the grand scale for an example. " 'What if my whole life has really been wrong?' " asks

Tolstoy's Ivan Ilyich. The "very justification of his life held him fast and prevented his moving forward, and it caused him the most torment of all." That's *hard,* as Faustus said of the divine laws, but *The Lonely Crowd* can reassure you that Ivan Ilyich's predicament need not be yours. Ivan, we read there, was an "inside dopester." Do not be an inside dopester and the laws will soften for you.

But if I should think that mad old Tolstoy meant you and me to see ourselves in Ivan and to believe that only in death could we transcend the already fatal formation of our lives— then, after the private shudder is mastered, I would note that such an idea of transcendence is not to be found on sale in the non-fiction on our Better Book counters.

Suppose that Alan Harrington, whose central moral image of "the crystal palace"* is lifted from Dostoevsky's *Notes from the Underground,* had also taken the thorny paradox of that story, had pictured himself as being "a spiteful man" like the Dostoevskian narrator who wants to stick his tongue out at *any and all* enduring palaces of the ideal. What foundation would subsidize a book by a spiteful man? What sane publisher would sponsor it?

But, with the spite removed from the original formula of the idea, Harrington's book lies comfortably on a Procrustean bed that could only reach the knees and elbows of Dostoevsky's terrifying riddle.

Suppose the author of *The Lonely Crowd* had identified his ideal of *autonomy* as *immorality.* Nietzsche says proudly enough that "autonomous and moral are mutually exclusive terms." That kind of pride is no more saleable than spite.

Suppose that Mills had based *The Causes of World War III* on the hard thesis that it is already too late to prevent the holocaust. (He says it isn't if enough of us avoid the pitfalls of the tragic view. If we "transcend" ourselves.)

Unsaleable.

Unsaleable first of all to the keepers of the Procrustean bed —editors, publishers, and foundations. But no doubt they are

---

* *Life in the Crystal Palace*

right in assuming, too, that untrimmed ideas are unsaleable to that public for whom they act as entrepreneurs. How many people would pay to go to bed with an idea bigger than themselves? It would be undignified, and to pay for the privilege of yielding dignity has become unthinkable, has it not?

By noting certain exclusions, then, we may infer that the style common to the books of popular sociology is one in which a premium is placed on communication—*after* certain great ideas that were once or somewhere communicable among men have become unthinkable. In turn this means that communication tends to be the sounding of already familiar signals (shibboleths or slogans flattering the preconceptions of the book buyer) rather than an attempt to reveal what is generally unknown in our novel situation. It is symptomatic of the wish to communicate at all costs that certain illustrations, allusions, and authorities have been kept in service in most of the books I am talking about. The novel *Kitty Foyle* becomes a tired old work horse while a hundred better novels about life in these states are never drawn upon at all. "The Protestant Ethic" (hiss!), Dr. Dichter (the Fu Manchu of Motivational Research), *1984* (otherwise known as the Book of Revelations), and well-surveyed Park Forest keep reappearing like popular recipes in the cookbooks issued by various publishers. One is not surprised to find in *The Status Seekers* the same less than oracular quote from Saint George Orwell's *Coming Up for Air* that Mills used within the first few pages of *White Collar*. But it might be really surprising to find any of them tackling—for example— Faulkner's story "Golden Land" or Dreiser's novel *The Bulwark* in discussing the history of conscience in twentieth century America.

Is there, in the present system by which we disseminate ideas, an iron law to the effect that success in communicating what no one needs very much to be told means obscuring what is truly needed? I don't know. But I think it unreasonable to expect, in this situation, that we will soon find a book of social analysis in which a concept like *transcendence* has more scope than C. Wright Mills gives it. (I believe that Mills intends the term to mean "working harder for peace and social justice."

That is, of course, a decent idea as well as a saleable one. But it is also a fair example of what confirms and narrows the secularization that he announces and, at his convenience, deplores.)

If such limits to the style of thinking as I have suggested are indeed the broadest we can expect in this field, the individual reader is left the task of separating, with less than common tolerance, what is wholesome there from the cheap pardons. Salvage depends on rejecting out of hand the merely pious pretense that every book "on the side of the angels" has power to heal the anxieties to which it is addressed.

Surely it must be plain that the anti-huckster huckster is no more an ally in the good old cause than the plain huckster. That the former has no tangible goods to sell does not mean that he is disinterested. If you get a sound pair of shoes in the bargain, it may be better to "buy beautiful feet" (*The Hidden Persuaders*) at the behest of some journeyman advertiser than to buy from a superficial critic the conviction that now you know where to look for the hidden persuasions.

Vance Packard, like some of the others I have mentioned, has been to the great feast of social science jargon and stolen the scraps. He will cry (more like the Summoner of the *Canterbury Tales* than the Pardoner, perhaps) "depth," "manipulation," and "status claim" in a most entertaining if unenlightening way. Between scaring you with how awfully much Dr. Dichter knows about you and reassuring you with his own *dichter-freiheit*, he will take you a very short trip for your money. I think he is fun when he gets off a line like "The New England aristocrat clings to his cracked shoes through many re-solings and his old hat." You can hardly buy "your Declaration of Independence," as the publishers advertised it, cheaper than by forking out for *The Status Seekers*.

Spectorsky's *The Exurbanites* is entertaining, too, and funny by intent. Spectorsky knows that the language and the posture of the social scientist can be structured into an amusing artifice. *The Exurbanites* is a new kind of novel without a hero, swift, satiric, detached, laying no particular claim to realism, but affording a considerable measure of aesthetic satisfaction.

It seems to me, though, that we can take *The Organization Man* by William H. Whyte, Jr., as seriously as it asks to be taken. Its opening definition of "the Protestant Ethic" on which the author must have intended to structure his thesis is, seriously, a stunning piece of social history-into-journalism legerdemain. I presume that his definition and "authority" for it were squeezed from Max Weber's *The Protestant Ethic and the Spirit of Capitalism.*

From large scholarship and an at least fruitful bias, Weber tried to show "whose intellectual child" was the rational thought of capitalism. There is absolutely no question of a "chicken or the egg" riddle in Weber's essay. But Whyte recklessly tries to riddle with the truth, writing, "Whether the Protestant Ethic preceded capitalism, as Max Weber argued, or whether it grew up as a consequence. . . ." Which latter alternative must mean, if it means anything, that the Spirit of Capitalism spaketh and said: "Do not commit adultery . . . sell whatever thou hast and give to the poor and thou shalt have treasure in heaven."

Milton, Weber, Jesus Christ, Thou shouldst be living at this hour, when a little education has become so permissive a thing!

Still, it may be carping to point out that Whyte started to build his edifice on the sands of a misrepresentation. Most of his opinions would seem to be a matter of taste rather than a consequence of principle or reason, and hence so lacking in fundamental coherence as to make a skeletal thesis unnecessary. When he discovers for himself that the material he has chosen contradicts what he wants to show, he says (p. 183, Anchor ed.) that he is "happy" it does. Could anyone ask for a softer sell than that? He has a lot of ideas that all men of good will in his position would certainly wish to espouse—like, all the colleges are going to hell because there's a bunch of educationalist nuts down on the liberal arts; like, you have no real privacy in an architectural monstrosity such as Park Forest; like, a man mustn't let any one organization take over his soul. You may not agree with Whyte's recollection that when he got out of college in 1939 the world scene was much brighter than it is in our organized times, but if you're an organization man who feels that his crystal palace is just an air-conditioned bureaucracy after all, you're bound to like Whyte's earnest admonition to "fight."

It must be reported that he qualifies his inspirational cry. You must fight—but not too hard.

Perhaps what the Moloch corporations needed was a sort of spiritually tasteful gymnasium where a man could go a few fast rounds, work up a nice sweat, and not show any marks afterward. Perhaps, in *The Organization Man,* they've got one.

Radix malorum est conformitas! One of the motives for decrying the general conformity of Americans is—as any waiting-room spread of popular magazines will evidence—to help the great mass-media artists behind the scenes sell "non-conformist" personalities: Jack Paar, Alexander King, Jack Kerouac, Mike Wallace, Mort Sahl, Joseph Welch, Marlon Brando. In *The Lonely Crowd* we read, "Surely the great mass-media artists, including the directors, writers, and others behind the scenes who 'create' and promote the artists, make an important contribution to autonomy." If any other contemporary guiding force receives equal praise in the book, I am sorry to say I did not find it, though travel agents, hotel men, resort directors, and interior decorators are conceded potentially comparable virtue. "My effort . . . has been directed to closing the gap generally believed to exist between high culture and mass culture," the author says. When I saw in which direction he meant to close this same gap I ran back to my peer-group—friends and neighbors—begging "Other-direct me." That Reisman is serious in his valuation of these on- and off-scene heroes of culture seems to be suggested by his persistent habit of descending from skillfully managed and colorful generalities to illustrate the particulars of American life as they were shown in some formula film.

"It's the inner life that counts," E. M. Forster used to say. And he used to say, "Only connect." But I think the glazed vocabulary of *The Lonely Crowd* precludes a connection between the inner life (be it only stupid pain or angry frustration) and the social gesture. "The inner-directed person has early incorporated a psychic gyroscope. . . ." The other-directed person's "control equipment, instead of being like a gyroscope, is like a radar." Certain colleges "turn out" more artists and scientists than others.

The point of mentioning these mechanically derived metaphors is not to show that Reisman mistakes symbol for substance. He says, "The metaphor of the gyroscope . . . must not be taken literally. . . . The inner-directed man . . . can receive and utilize certain signals from outside. . . . His pilot is not quite automatic."

The point is that this style (of language, of thought) meshes flawlessly with the styles educed by advertising or the mass media generally, and is absolutely inconsistent with the traditional conceptual language of humane letters. This style is perfect for adding a flourish of highbrow interpretation to Jerry Wald's movie derivation from *The Sound and the Fury* but would be helpless as a Univac if engaged to interpret Faulkner's original.

No wonder that progressively Riesman must find us progressively apathetic. To paraphrase Mannheim, "His style measures what it is able to measure rather than what we want to know about." His thought, encumbered in such language, cannot accommodate the pathos of real people any more than it can imply their individual wisdom, folly, or resentment of the institutions that have failed to shape a spiritual life for them. He contrives a sociology of wind-up toys—very ingenious, but ingenuity is easier when responsibility to the subject is cast aside.

He builds his case on an appearance of apathy that many have noted. But is our well-fed, over-stimulated, frustrated populace apathetic? Could it be? Or is it only unresponsive when the wrong demands are made of it? It is a terrible and dangerous thing to judge Philomela by her silences.

If we looked through another peephole than Riesman's we might see that *out there,* on the invisible end of the TV circuits, in the voiceless pits of theaters, or reading *The Lonely Crowd,* people are making cruel fun of "the great artists." They may be out there sharpening their gully knives.

Probably not. No cry of "Out with your gully knives!" is likely to be heard from a citizenry outraged by the thinness of its cultural soup.* Spiteful children may scribble the signature of their disaffection on the posters by the masters of the popular arts, but overt rebellions of good or evil are hardly conceivable at this late date. Even the famous revolt in Hungary prospered (if that is the right word) far more as propaganda in the mass media than it did in the streets of Budapest.

Individual or collective, rebellion is almost certain to be subsumed in the machinery of power where ideas, like actions, are compounded into a homogeneity that has already outlawed a host of precious human possibilities.

The only chance of transcending this homogeneity must surely be in discovering the extent to which it has deprived our individual lives of significance, facing up to our peculiar tragedy. I believe that C. Wright Mills knows that this must be done. "It is one great task of social studies to describe the larger economic and political situation in terms of its meaning for the inner life and external career of the individual," he wrote some years ago in *White Collar*. I think he has made large contributions to this task. But I think his very anger, his well-meaning zeal, prevent him from seeing it through. He turns back and minimizes the task he defines—because he is afraid that men will sit down and fold their hands in despair if they perceive the tragedy and futility of their lives.

I do not think that is so. My experience says it is not so. Yeats's "Lapis Lazuli" says it is not so, and on the level of simple factual statement about the nature of man (aesthetic considerations aside) I trust what Yeats says and do not trust Mills.

Yeats says that men, "if worthy their prominent part in the play will not break up their lines to weep" whatever the prospects of their practical success. I think that order of truth explains and encourages all men who, in their different ways, may be trying to prevent another war or the further impoverishment of our social life. On the other hand, Mills can only

---

* This was obviously written before the Great American Riots began, before the children of affluence took to the streets with the Negroes. Now "apathy" has ben exposed for what it truly was during the Fifties.

encourage those who agree with his program and can explain, at best, only a few dubiously practical steps for achieving it.

It does not help to call those who admit or express the tragic view "the literary counterpart of the cult of objectivity in the social sciences"—as Mills does, making the latter sound worse than it is—or to say paraphrastically, "they are betrayed by what is false within them." This is to make bad poetry out of good and leads straight on to the rant, self-righteousness, and the internal contradictions that mar his books. (For an example of the latter—he tries to pin "responsibility" on the "irresponsible men" of the power elite, an undertaking that would require not only a more precise language than his but a theory of power in the modern state which he fails to provide.)

In *The Causes of World War III* he says, "To ask and answer the question 'What is to be done?' is not enough. We must also specify who is to do it." That seems reasonable enough, but then, proceeding as if to specification, he specifies —the United States. Following this specification which is no specification at all, he offers eighteen "guidelines" by which it, they, or we might press for peace. Among them is this ". . . the United States should . . . offer to share fully the costs of . . . an international fleet of airliners for the use of scientists, intellectuals, and artists. . . ." That's a delightful prescription, but I see little more reason to suppose that it would foster peace than that the United States or any of its specific branches or groups of citizens would make such an offer.

The emptiness of his argument at such turns serves only to discredit his thesis that reason can master fate and reminds us again that reason can never seize remote goals until it has mastered the proximate.

Even so, there is a genuine and stalwart poetry in Mills at his best. The poetry is in the pity if nowhere else. And if one is exasperated by his growl and overstatement ("Macy's hurts Mr. Mills," someone said), it seems likely that his anger defines the area in which we may hope to claim our transcendence, even when his thought does not.

243450

How Beautiful Art
Came to America

A great part of the first-rate cultural life one can have in our time and place is available to us as a result of a trick we have developed of parodying the official, academic, or mass cultural manifestations which dominate us by their volume, and which are as patently second-rate as they are lively and ubiquitous. We go to the movies, for example, and are satisfied there, not by an innocent acceptance of what we see, but by seeing the impure product through a system of corrective and refractive references that permit us to see simultaneously an action and, in contrapuntal parody, the enactment of the convention which has dictated the action's incredible course. The mind receives a divided image—one part of it is a visual image of, perhaps, a man kissing a woman, the other part is of a complex, familiar code which decrees how far the woman's mouth will appear to open under this impact. A movie kiss becomes a believable representation of human actions only in the juxtaposition of the two halves of this image, that is, only insofar as we employ the aesthetic and intellectual method of relativism which is parody.

Fortunately we have been trained in the practices of subtle parody, not always humorous. With what has been widely assimilated from Freud, Picasso, the Dadaists, and Joyce, it is not a task for a genius to adapt oneself to take nourishment and meaning from a multitude of offerings which, taken straight, would be corruptive or at best without force of any kind. By parody we are free of commitment to the camp of those who believe what they see at the movies and from the position of the pure who don't go because they can't believe. Through the range of the arts parody keeps us clear of idolatry or destructive cynicism. Its business is the rearrangement of contexts. A genial parodist once added a mustache to the Mona Lisa and all at once we could see this painting again without the silly effort of trying to imagine ourselves Renaissance Florentines or as species existing outside time. The mustache reminded us that here was a painting which had passed through certain corridors of history to exist now in a context of space and meaning accessible to contemporary minds, eyes, and hands.

That the *New Yorker,* where *Duveen* by S. N. Behrman originally appeared as a series of articles, traffics in many kinds of parody is one of the reasons why it is so pleasantly effective in establishing contexts for a multitude of expressions of our culture. Whether *New Yorker* parody really provides a corrective supplement to the raw image which serves it as a point of departure is, nonetheless, a question that requires asking even at the risk of spoiling the weekly fun. It is a question that bobs up whenever the pace of a typical *New Yorker* feature, like *Duveen,* slacks off enough to permit second thoughts.

Behrman's book is an account of the life and exploits of a supersalesman whose real commodity is conspicuous consumption, who dealt nominally in "masterpieces of art." Duveen established and satisfied in a gilt-edged selection of American millionaires a taste for "the Old Masters." In Behrman's bluntest words, "Duveen made the names familiar, and compelled a reverence for them because he extracted such overwhelming prices for them." His technique of extraction and the techniques of ritual resistance and ritual submission to his salesmanship demonstrated by Mellon, Huntington, Kress, etc., are the subject of the best comic passages of a book which is largely comedy. The story of how "The Blue Boy" came to America is a larking study in doltishness which at least deserves to be framed and hung in place of that sticky painting.

The attempt of a group of dealers to interest Henry Ford in becoming a collector during a lean period when their regular customers were disposing their money otherwise—paying income taxes perhaps—is also a biting vignette of big money operators. (Ford was greatly pleased with the reproductions in the catalog presented to him by the dealers, but, having these to look at, saw no reason for laying out a lot of cash for the originals.)

What we are shown finally is how, through Duveen's salesmanship and through the extravagances and dreams of glory of his customers, our country acquired vicariously that part of its taste which is represented by the National Gallery. Here is the material of a parody with which the value of the acquisitions housed there could be tried and made viable. It is more than *interesting* to discover the processes by which national museums and the authority of certain works of art have been created. It is a necessary part of seeing them.

But Behrman resolutely refuses to admit that the meaning and value of the art that came into our possession through Duveen are relative. It is only as a joke that he will speak of these paintings as "Duveens"—and one feels an implied insistence that this joke be laughed at in an O.K. and patriotic way. After all, these paintings were done by Raphael, Rembrandt, Titian, Lawrence, Reynolds, and no one had better laugh at them (or spit on the flag) because they were living, breathing Old Masters and therefore not in any corpuscle, fingernail, brushstroke, or quality of spirit inventions of any Joseph Duveen, living, dead, or invented.

These whimsicals can be pretty solemn types when their impulse to make fun is exhausted, and so with Behrman. He seems to accept without equivocation the principles which are funny when they are guiding stars for Duveen's funny clients— that price is the sure criterion (rather than a component) of value, and that authenticity, in the narrow sense of authorship of a work, is a base on which price ought to be established. When, rarely, there is a reference to standards broader than these, it is to the opinion of "experts" who have pronounced this or that work to be "great" or "the finest" at some point on its passage through Duveen's selling apparatus. Terms like "infallible taste," "the real thing," and "refined" crop up when the author wants to speak seriously of Duveen's commodity.

"Duveen," he says, "transformed the American taste in art."
"He not only educated the small group of collectors who were
his clients but created a public for the finest works of the
masters of painting." "He forced American collectors to accu-
mulate great things, infused them with a fierce pride in col-
lecting, and finally got their collections into museums, making
it possible for the American people to see a large share of
the world's most beautiful art without having to go abroad."
Not only can the American people see "beautiful art"—with
Behrman's encouragement they can marvel at how much it cost,
can be assured of beauty by referring it to price.

Which is to say that Behrman has labored amusingly to
get back where his cast of characters started from, and the book
is a pseudo-parody, meaning only, perhaps, that people are
funny. The total effect is weirdly like what we might get if a
verbally talented J. P. Morgan had written *The Theory of the
Leisure Class* or if *A Modest Proposal* had been written by a
cannibal.

Looking for an Archetype

To my beginning students I say: Compose in skeins and rhythms.

Initiating a course of instruction by the utterance of such a rune is to put myself in a perilous relation with young people who are paying good money and spending the delicate potentials of their youth listening to me.

After telling them that I will show them how to compose "in skeins and rhythms" I have to leap like mad to keep them from concluding I merely want to be cute in a professorial way. Perhaps they conclude that anyhow, and then I have to dance for a semester or a year undoing this all-important first impression of theirs.

I had better untangle the knot, because I have *something* to teach them, whether I can teach them what they have expected or not. Perhaps they enroll expecting me to teach them "to write" and I can't do that. In my role as editor of their stories, poems, or essays, I might indeed be able to show them how to clarify and improve what they have written. And that is not unimportant; for part of the task of writing is editorial. The writer has to learn how to become his own editor, and I can show students how the editorial functions are performed.

But the real thing in writing—in the practice of any art, of course—is *composition,* the bringing together, the arrangement of material in significant sequence and relationship, the selection of things that go together, the perception of true relevance.

Composition—that splendid, wonderful word has been filched away from us teachers of writing, tied elsewhere in the curriculum, locked away from us like the princess in the tower, guarded by the fierce old dragon of professional literary education, who assigns us to and pays us for teaching something called "creative writing." I wish I didn't teach "creative writing." I wish I taught composition, except that then I wouldn't be paid as much, for composition classes are often taught by graduate students. Some of them, I know, are taught marvelously well; but the official assumption is that what is taught in such classes is the correct formation of sentences and perhaps paragraphs, and perhaps the construction of those military term papers that really consist of one file card pasted to the bottom of another and then transcribed on a typewriter. Which is a sorry substitute for real composition.

But the titles assigned to classes and teachers are not very important after all. So, in the little time I have with them, I try to tell my students something of how and why one composes in skeins and rhythms. I say to them—and saying is only the beginning of pedagogy, we agree—that as writers we must compose thus because as humans, as consciousness implicated with time, we compose ourselves (or are composed) thus. From the beginning of our individual lives, nature pulls on this thread or another of our being, knots it or weaves it, and then lets it go for a while before the rhythm of pulling begins again. The mythic figures that form the structure of our consciousness appear in their turns and say, like the girls and boys we meet after a while, "Plant you now and dig you later."

Our lives are made of various skeins—perhaps not very many, after all—that are tugged for a while, loosened, and tugged again in rhythms we try to comprehend and to some extent control or put ourselves in harmony with. One of the means by which we hope to exercise a magical control or a religious acceptance of our lives is art. In the art of writing each of us attempts to bring together and arrange in sequence and relationship what has been planted in our consciousness by its long elaboration in the passage of time. We try to give— a little and for a little while—the kind of willful composition to the materials that nature will compose anyway. We want, in our heightening of the natural process, a sense of possession, a sense of participation, and even—the most human wish of all —a sense that we have outwitted the implacability of time. That we have made a work which will endure. What is more touching for those of us who write—all of us who write—than Shakespeare's lines:

> Not marble nor the gilded monuments of princes
> Shall outlast this powerful rhyme.

We try to compose a work—as nature composes consciousness and time—in order to make nature stay a while, a moment or a day, or longer than marble or gilded monuments.

II

The teacher of writing offers himself as an example to his students—which would be shameful and unsporting if he were unable to expose himself as a man writing but only as an elder who has had some degree of attested success. What he has written is a poor exhibit for students until he can let them understand the processes of his life out of which, from time to time, the printed testimony spilled. The movement of the mind is always toward greater self-consciousness, and this, in himself, is what the teacher tries to reveal.

In his riper years he ought to say, "What I did twenty or thirty years ago that seemed, even to me, so blind, has turned out to be not altogether blind. It was not only purposeful, but, as I now see, part of my awareness not yet aware that it was aware." There is a tendency to incorporate into consciousness that which it would have been impudent to call consciousness at an earlier time. To encourage the student to strain forward in anticipation of the time when the "accidents" of his life will arrange themselves in meaning is perhaps to give him something a good deal more valuable than a knowledge of correct grammar or structure.

So I'm encouraged to tell again—I have told it before—a fragmentary story of how a novel was composed by and for me. My excuse is that I know more now about how I composed it than when I put it on paper and sent it to my publisher. (Another way of saying the same thing is to say that I am still composing it.) It did not cease as a process of my imaginative life when it was printed. It goes on as a telling, a rhythmic repeat and continuation, altering and diminishing as it paradoxically grows. Something of mine and something of me that has no certain beginning or end.

Pretty Leslie is, as any categoricalist can plainly see, a naturalistic novel. It is psychological, sociological, contemporary, strongly but assymetrically plotted, and more loosely organized verbally than any other novel I have written. These are unarguable characteristics, which mean very little to me. One good reviewer said it was an audacious attempt to rewrite *Madame Bovary* for our times. An equally perceptive reviewer said that in composing the image of the heroine I had sketched the contemporary anti-type of Emma Bovary, a kind of reversed mirror image of her. Both of these observations are true to a degree.

Both are bewildering to me because they predicate a kind of starting point which I hardly recognize at all. They postulate as beginning what could only have appeared, even to the author, very far along in the process of composition. But most bewildering because they challenge me to ask myself what the real beginning was.

I can no longer believe any answer that says the novel was begun at any discernible point in time. I am going to say—and try to find out whether I believe it or not—that it began with an Egyptian relief which I found reproduced in an art book several weeks after I had begun to type the first draft of the novel.

The sculptured relief shows the stark figure of a hawk. Below it is a short, horizontal line. Below that there is a serpent, whose lines repeat the lines of the hawk's back. Nothing more.

What shows in this double image, divided so majestically with the kind of line we find in numerical fractions, is a separation and a juxtaposition of a primitive and an evolved form. The serpent is primitive—a spine with a head. In the bird, wings and legs have been added to the basic form of the serpent.

In the intensely troubled and productive weeks before I came on this photograph of the Egyptian decoration, I had been going frequently to the quaint, dear little museum of natural history in a building called MacBride Hall at the University of Iowa. I was writing a novel and I was up there trying to see my characters. I stood outside the glass cases there in the dim, religious light from old-fashioned skylights, peering at ravens and swans, condors and wolves, nighthawks and zebras—plus a pair of lions that a local clothing merchant had brought home from a safari to Africa and had given, for as long as they lived, to the Iowa City zoo.

As I say, I was trying to see my characters among these stuffed creatures, though I had been reading about them for years in newspapers, talking and listening to others, accumulating notes in my notebook, projecting their anguishes and lust into my legal and adulterous carnality, and raising them in my love toward a condition where compassion was involuntary. I saw them there . . . incompletely. There is, let me tell you, something incredibly seductive about the curving inner thigh of a stuffed zebra. That made me burn for my heroine, Leslie Daniels.

There is, as Auden tells us in a poem, something unbearably pathetic about the long lines and ceremonial mane of a lion, particularly one that has been brought to Iowa City, Iowa, by old Mr. Bremer, the clothing store owner. Lions had been in my dreams for years. In one of my earliest memories of childhood I had been frightened by the reproduction of Rosa Bonheur's painting of a lion's head. (I had cried out, according to my mother, " 'ion eatee.") Alone in the stifling museum, time was drastically discounted for me. No doubt a number of useful details were gathered in my hours there.

But when I saw the Egyptian relief, it confirmed that the thing I had seen most impressively in the museum was the fateful relation between the skeleton of a bird and the skeleton of a snake. (Those incredible, yellowed whites against a dusty black background, behind glass.) I had seen that the spine and skull of the snake were visibly intact within the equipage of ribs, wingbones, and leg structure of the more complex creature.

These things had been before my eyes, floating on the surface of my mind. I was, so to speak, "let in on" their meaning when I saw the Egyptian decoration.

About the same time—this was while I was actually typing a draft of the novel and naturally very deeply involved with its language and the structuring of scenes and movements of action—I was intensely scanning and studying reproductions of Titian's painting, and in this becoming aware of something halfway between iconography and what, in modern terms, we would call the design of the pictures. I began to think of this intermediate formation as "stagecraft"—a banal enough term designating for me the disposition of figures and objects, each having a certain symbolic and literal quality, over the canvas in such a way as to suggest a temporal sequence—one thing or combination of things *following* others, though obviously they existed in spatial simultaneity. I felt an exciting disturbance, as if on the verge of discovering a new way to apprehend time.

I was particularly fascinated by a long, horizontal picture of Titian's called the Pardo Venus. I made a copy of it, because copying is one way of looking at or reading anything, and because copying a painting—in which you must put in one element *after* another—is a way of breaking up the simultaneity you see in a finished canvas. In this process of study I began to see something in the painting that vaguely (at any rate usefully) coincided with my apprehension of the Egyptian ideogram. The painting was divided almost as radically as the bas relief and to the same effect. On one side are the civilized, clothed figures of huntsmen and courtiers. On the other a faun is going for a naked Venus. And in the more complex, evolved formation the primitive is fatefully preserved.

At this point I might declare that I had discovered in the painting and the Egyptian relief the archetype which was to govern the structure of the novel, that in seeing them I clarified my intuition about my heroine and what must happen to her. That I saw the relationship of tension between sexuality and personality. ("Leslie lives in fear of her civilized self being annihilated by something wild, lawless, animalistic that she senses within her," as reviewer Robert Alter put it.)

Well and good. It is a commonplace that one's intentions clarify as one proceeds with a task, that writing is as much a process of mining down to a sub-stratum of truth as it is building up a structure that will proclaim it. By my preliminary work I had uncovered the archetypal pattern that had always been there, then had recognized that archetype of my consciousness, reflected as in a mirror, when I stared at the two works of visual art. That explanation seems pat, and in accordance with what we have been taught by contemporary psychology.

But how to account *exactly* for the strong sense that the archetypal image of primitive and complex forms was coming into existence at the same time I was perceiving it? I had no sense that the archetype had *always* been in my mind or that it was altogether *timeless*. On the other hand, it was plainly not a brand new creation. The archetype, as I recognized it, existed in time. But *where* in time? Dating it, saying it existed at a particular time and not at another was impossible. It appeared to me that it continued in time (had continued for centuries, if you like) but without an even density of reality. It appeared to me that I had known throughout my life, in infancy and green adolescence, exactly what I knew when I understood the pattern my novel must follow. But without the same density of awareness.

Which comes first in the work of the imagination—a governing idea, an image or equation, or the material which will be the flesh of the idea? Supposing there are skeins of experience or of predisposition running evenly through each of our lives or through many lives. What determines the rhythm of attention one pays to each of these, picking it up for a while, letting it go, and attending to it again? And how can I say that my novel began with the archetype of serpent and bird when it would be equally as convincing to say that it began with the attention I paid to some stories in the midwestern newspapers of 1948 and 1949?

In that period I was reading about a juicy murder case. The pretty wife of a young pediatrician had got involved in an affair with a shabby sort of salesman whom she had met while working in a defense plant during the war. Her husband finally met the salesman in a hotel room in Iowa and in a quarrel took his knife away from him and stabbed him to death.

From the time I read these newspaper stories, I had known this story was mine—that is, it was one of the things I must write about when and as I could. I don't mean, merely, that the circumstances of the case presented themselves as material that I could use effectively. It must have been rather that I grasped the pattern of necessity from which these circumstances had emerged. But how would I have recognized this unless I already had as part of the structure of my consciousness, to use a Jungian term, the ideogram of serpent and bird? (A figure which represents not only the different status and social appearance of the two men in the case, but also the doubleness in the woman which would respond to both, as she did in marriage and in adultery.)

This idea of the doubleness involved in a sexual triangle or the doubleness of women is nothing either complex or new. It is in every sense of the word a commonplace—and I might satisfy a certain kind of literary historical curiosity if I said offhandedly that I got the formula from reading *Lear* when I was a sophomore in college. I took seriously Lear's statement:

Down from the waist they are Centaurs
Though women all above:
But to the girdle do the gods inherit
Beneath is all the fiends';
There's hell, there's darkness, there's the sulphurous pit,
Burning, scalding, stench, consumption. . . .

But I don't know how seriously I took (or was taken by) this when I read it at eighteen or nineteen; and the dreamwork of composition depends almost altogether, I suppose, on the quantitative dynamism of the encounter with an idea. Lightly we brush an immense swarm of ideas, a multitude of experiences. Some of these stick. Something imbeds and keeps working. Most goes past without leaving a trace. Composition is not only the exploitation of what sticks; it is also the effort to find out why just this thing and not something else is relevant. Or becomes relevant.

Perhaps the quote from *Lear* was indeed part of what was being put together by me and in me which would presently fit itself to the Egyptian image of hawk and serpent. (Which, indeed, I must have seen much earlier in my life in and around my dreams and fears of the outdoor privy we used when I was a small child in Sheldahl, Iowa. "The sulphurous pit, Burning, scalding, stench, consumption. . . ." I used to dream, quite literally, of snakes in the stinking pit below the wooden seat. Emerging hurriedly I used to look up for the pigeons that circled above the structure and the barn which it adjoined.)

I think the skeins which came together much later in the drafting of my novel were being composed into elaborations of the simple pattern—were preparatory sketches for it, searching for it in the stuff of my life as a sculptor looks for his figure in the stone—at least as long ago as my years in Sheldahl. I don't think my mind contained the archetype then, but was being tugged toward it like a compass needle tugged North.

When, in 1948 and 1949 I read the pitiable stories of the pediatrician who killed his wife's lover, one thing about it seemed more painfully familiar than anything else. Though he was known to his community and his patients as an entirely gentle man, he had in his childhood in Texas shot and killed a playmate—deliberately, as far as one could make out from the newspaper accounts.

Why should this horror be so familiar? It is my firm, waking conviction that I have never killed anyone in my life this far. And yet, at various periods in my life I have had recurrent dreams of being a child and having killed a playmate. The body is buried somewhere, usually in excrement, and I have tried to pass off the crime by an excruciating show of composure in the face of a circle of suspicions. In reading about the pediatrician's childhood crime, I was reading about myself as I knew myself in dreams. Even in my most rational hours of waking composure I could not—and cannot—escape this duplication of his fate, since it appears that my mind's effort to distinguish between the self my dreams know and the waking self is just like the distinction he had to make between his adult self and the child he had been.

In cogitating this character it seemed to me—this is what Blake would call a memorable fancy—that in him the child had remained intact within the more elaborate structure of the adult as the snake, which is all spine, remains intact within the complexity of the bird. The paradoxical guilts that express the innocence of childhood are not superseded by our adult conduct but are incorporated into it—different, antithetical, fearsome, but yet indistinguishable. In this maddening division within unity—which seems to have nothing at all to do with schizophrenia or split personality as these are clinically defined—I saw the fate of my chief male character.

After reading these newspaper stories, through the 1950's I composed a manageable, rationalized view of women. I wasn't doing this with a notebook in hand, in order to fill in the blank space in a novel as children use their crayolas to color between the lines of a coloring book. I was trying to compose an understanding for the classical reasons—to save my life, to get along with women in the world. What I learned, what I came to know, had no date. There was no moment or hour when I fully and neatly possessed, to use with precision, the knowledges gained in that decade. It is only now, in these reflections, that I see in my relations with two women with whom I was intensely, destructively in love the hieroglyphic pattern of inner division, expressed in their responses to me and other men. I did not use them in my novel. I used the novel to compose my present view of them.

I am not going into the least detail about my experiences with these two; but I will cite one encounter with a female which I found paradigmatic and which I used, almost intact, early in the novel as a controlling figure.

One cold day in the early sixties I took my two-year-old daughter to the city park. We took some bread to feed the ducks. The sight of the actual ducks darting and hissing like snakes around our feet in the icy water frightened her. She was afraid to let the bread go out of her hand to them. She saw—how else could I put it?—she saw the serpent in the bird and had to cling to what was hers on pain of a violation she was unprepared to accept. But, as we walked away, getting farther and farther from the pond, she began to throw bits of the bread back toward where it would have been welcomed.

In her belated, useless gesture I saw a bit of ready-made. Almost blatantly this is the revelation of an orgasm pattern structured on a fearful hesitation. I set it in as such at the beginning of Chapter Six.

III

I tell my students that characters in fiction are, and must be, composites drawn from the diverse observations of living people. And then they ask the intelligent question: Yes, but how do you choose from all the bits and pieces of natural detail that memory gives you those few details which *belong?*

I tell them they must keep notebooks in which the various skeins of interest or compulsion which they are slowly composing into a design will be recorded as they lengthen. And they ask: But what, of all that one might put in a notebook, should I put in mine?

The formal answer I give is that there must be a "governing principle of selection" in preparing composites, in filling out a section in one's personal notebook. But of course such jargon is not very helpful, and what I am saying here is an attempt to be a little bit concrete in defining what may be a governing sign, or an equation, or the structure of apprehension around which material can be clustered in relevant bunches. I am saying that I found I had been composing through all my life a kind of "proto-novel," a consistency within my experience which repeated rhythmically and finally became tractable when I recognized the absurdly simple sign of the serpent and bird. In some sense the novel was made before I began to put it on paper. At any rate, much of the work on it had been done (and I certainly do not mean, by saying this, that I had, in any simple way, observed, read, or rationalized a story; I am talking about processes of composition that go deep as life).

About the actual writing, I want to say something a little shocking. I consider that as no more and no less than a re-enactment of actual encounters with actual women. (I have an aphorism: The thing being described is the thing being enacted.) The writing about Leslie Daniels was a repetition of affairs and marriages of the last twenty years. Presiding over the physical act of writing there were all the reiterations of consciousness that occur as the by-product of a passion in full swing. Day by day I tried to decipher Leslie's moves as before I had tried to interpret F— and M—.

When, in a rhythmic repetition of a passion, you see what you saw, then you have a period in the unceasing life of the imagination when you can produce a work, a novel, or a drama. When you are making a work, there is no easy distinction between what you are using (as of inert material and acquired skill) and what you are doing (making new shapes according to patterns which are by no means new). Everything is grist for the mill. I said I went to the museum of natural history and used what I saw there. I used the Egyptian ornament that I came upon at that time.

There are a profusion of bird and snake images in the novel. (I have no interest in counting them. I did not consciously place them.) Leslie Daniels, the doctor's wife, is in some sense of the term a bird, until her plumage is stripped from her. There is a neat liaison between chapters 19 and 20 accomplished with the detail of feathers from Leslie's dead parakeet. Don Patch, the mean little adulterer, is jokingly referred to as a snake. And so on.

But, as we know, such play with language and detail in a novel is mere froth on the wave, the frivolity that academic critics like to play with. It is the large movements and the rhythm of the crests that count. Language must be shaped to mark and define them, of course. This is its chief function in fiction. It is the fusion of language with the large conception that shows best the presence of the governing idea or pattern in a novel with a naturalistic surface.

The passages I want to quote here are not offered as examples of my "style" but in the hopes that they may show in their brevity the imprint of what I saw in the ideogram of snake and bird.

The first marks the moment when the doubleness of Leslie's nature is first totally exposed. It is not the moment of her first orgasm, by any means, but this is, you might say, the orgasm that counts, the moment when the intact child in her emerges into equal partnership with the plumed wife of the doctor:

> . . . it was as if an unknown—perhaps never created—island in the darkness of her body began to be identified. It was a nothing, taught by the rote of pain to *know itself,* to know of its own blind cunning that it must survive at the expense of her body and mind. Clawed like the symbol for cancer, it scratched for its survival inside the smothering cave. It moved on ponderous, hairy feet toward the source of light, lumbering like an elephant on spidery, insufficient legs toward the destruction that created it. And was free, gasping its gratitude in gouts of venom, slobbering its monstrous tears at the mouth of the cave, rolling pinpoint eyes and blinking over a white landscape. From its chimerical throat bubbled moans of praise for the Creator, humility and incomprehension that something so uncouth had been drawn slimy from the clay and permitted to know itself. Its cry would not even be an ape cry for millions of years. It tried to sing its allellulia from beyond the history of male and female.

Then there is a time, considerably later, when her husband recognizes her in the same simple way I recognized her when I saw the Egyptian relief—divided in a fashion that he can never quite come to terms with in a single life or incarnation, the moment when he realizes she has two husbands, one of which his tragic past forbids him to be.

> He reached across her and turned on the bed lamp. Recoiling, he paused above her, leaning on one arm. He stared down into her face with such hatred that she closed her eyes.
>
> "God, I wish you'd kill me," she said. "If you knew, why didn't you whip me when you came home? I'm not

smart. You're my husband. You could have punished me. As much as I deserved."

What he sensed rising from her then, almost but not quite palpable as an odorous veil that wrapped his head, was her beastly submission. As if someone had struck him an enormous blow with a fist, nearly smashing the back of his head, he saw her as she had been—had always been—when she gave what she had never given him.

This is the simple core of the novel, embodying the "mathematical" formula of discrepancy that constitutes the tragedy. And also it is the core of what I have to say about the novel's composition, for in isolating it from its context I have shown exactly the governing formula which dictated the choice of all the material and details that went into it.

I haven't been and can't be precise about a moment when I was either unaware or first fully aware of this formula. Through a very long time there had been in my thought a sort of rhythm in which I came into more or less intense awareness of what I was doing. Somewhere the skein of awareness turned into a novel. It was made into a novel which was printed.

Composition, in the sense that I am talking about it, does not end there. That is merely the manufacture of a commodity, and as I get older I get less interested in and less impressed by "works" of art and more filled with wonder at the "working" of art.

For quite a long time after the publication of this novel the composition of its skeins was halted. Instead of knowing more about what it meant and what was in it, I knew less.

What I am doing now, in writing about it, is making a return to lines that I have left in darkness for quite a while. In looking at it thus again, I am considering the finished and manufactured book as mere data, mere *sign,* as I once considered the newspaper stories about the murder signs and data.

The novel is present and is gone. Each of us has only a few things to say or testify to, and however much we may write we are trying to come to terms with those incredibly simple and persistent formulas which govern us.

We know that a novel has many words, as a life has many episodes. A novel has a complex sort of stagecraft—as a Titian painting has a complex stagecraft compared to the simplicity of the Egyptian design I have been talking about. But perhaps all the episodes and elaboration are means by which we try to come to the simplicity of our own truth.

In *Wuthering Heights* Catherine Earnshaw says, "I've dreamt in my life dreams that have stayed with me ever after, and changed my ideas: they've gone through and through me, like wine through water and altered the colour of my mind." The writer working with naturalistic materials is aware of something from himself and beyond himself coloring those materials like wine in water. The work of composition is a kind of dream work moving always, and always incompletely, toward the point at which consciousness can isolate the coloring agent from the inert stuff it colors.

Through the production of all works of the imagination we struggle toward a kind of wakefulness where the principles of selection can be consciously controlled; where we can articulate them like laws or mathematical formulae. And still we are afraid of this termination. For when they are quite isolated from the bewilderment of appearances—when the novel can be reduced to aphorism—the results are excruciatingly banal. The meaning will have eluded us. We will have overrun it.

When I have finished composing my thoughts about sexuality and the human pair—of which the novel *Pretty Leslie* is an emblem of the middle of the journey—I can expect no wisdom beyond the great truisms that every child encounters.

To compose is simply to organize, now and then, each time for a little while, the multiplicity of experience around these core simplicities.

Friends and Characters

Everyone knows that novelists write "about real people," that, in one way or another, the raw factuality of the real world gets embedded in fiction, and that writers more often than not "have an actual person in mind" when they draw a fictional character. This element of reportage, exposure, or confession is tacitly accepted in most cases as part of the fictional game. Sometimes it amounts to a special bonus of fun. People like to have their pictures taken. They like to be in print and see their acquaintances there with them, all distorted from their common selves as in a funhouse mirror. They like to see, or suppose they see, how they come off in the measuring to which a novelist almost inevitably subjects them.

Sometimes, though, there are hurt feelings and no fun at all. Charges of malice and unfairness, not altogether beside the point, are made against the writer. If he has a modicum of tact and an instinct for self-preservation he is likely to maintain that he had no objective except artistic excellence and that the search for any resemblance to people living or dead in his work is, in itself, a slanderous imputation against his imaginative powers.

But when the game is played for mortal stakes, as it must be in serious fiction, there can arise a tragic conflict of interest between the honorable obligations of the writer and the legitimate self-esteem of the friends, family, and lovers who have been used without permission in the discharge of these self-imposed obligations. Hawthorne admonishes us to "show freely to the

world . . . some token by which the worst may be inferred."
Yet we still live in a society where scarlet letters are less avidly
coveted than those awarded for athletic prowess. There is the
famous case of the woman who was the original for Miriam
Leivers in *Sons and Lovers.* I have never been able to get it
quite straight whether she was martyred by her eventually well-
publicized exploitation in that book, or whether she was, in
some glorious fashion, a collaborator in bringing to birth its
terrible beauty.

Gripped by ecstatic conviction—in which Lawrence rested
to the end of his days, I suppose—the writer proceeds in faith
that the people whose anguish and embarrassment he borrows
for his fiction should want to be used as he is using them. That
is, their *best selves* would want it, even if their fearful, conventional voices protest a rape of their conventional good names.
The writer's mandate is, after all, the same as that of any
educator, healer, or leader. He must crack the shell of the
conventional image so the truer, better one can emerge. And
he must be the one to imagine and declare the measure by
which, in his writing, the loved ones will be measured. He can't
ask them to vote on whether or not they want to follow to the
promised land, because in their conventional bondage they dare
not even imagine the wilderness through which they must pass
on the way.

Thus the writer must reason. But on his off days, when he,
too, wakens to the inertia of reality, he hears the chiding, hurt
voices say, "Not everyone thinks the way you do." Voices tell
him that in his presumptuous dream he has committed common
libels. He has infringed on someone else's right to account for
himself, privately or publicly.

Hurt in his turn, the writer insists he has done what writers
have always done. He quotes Burns—"A child's amang ye,
takin' notes, an' faith, he'll print it." To which his sore, involuntary original might well respond by quoting *The Aspern
Papers* to the effect that he is "a publishing scoundrel."

Sometimes, of course, these contentions come to litigation.
For many months I have been an outside observer of the case of
a novel whose publication has been held up by a legal wrangle.

When I first read the novel in manuscript—frankly unconcerned about whether or to what extent it was based on actual circumstance—I was struck by the way all its characters were radiated by the art and love of the presentation. Surely some of the characters stumbled this way and that off the paths of good conduct. They seemed in the world of the book no less precious for their errors.

But the measures of character within the book are, to some extent, in tragic opposition to the measures chosen or accepted by those who believe themselves disparagingly portrayed. I suppose that, as always when the law pronounces on literary ethics, the law will do the best it can. It is heartbreaking to think that in present circumstances it can't do very well.

Part of the trouble is that, with the best will in the world, the legal experts into whose hands the contention has come cannot look anywhere with confidence that an enlightened and humane consensus of literary intellectuals—let alone an intelligible doctrine—might illuminate the quandary. We are all in the dark. It is terribly hard for any decent man to draw the lines of tolerance in what must inevitably amount to an act of exposure.

There is apparently little value in recalling that the *roman a clef* is a traditional part of prose literature. The term itself sounds quaint to us now. We feel it belongs to a period of less bewildering social stratification and of more restricted candor in fiction. Once it provided a genteel cachet for the novel which was supposed—charmingly or for self-evident social objectives—to unlock the otherwise "untold story" of personages intended to be identified. Where the identification is coincidental and its resultant impact unpredictable, the painful shocks appear. I know a lot of splendid people who wouldn't mind being written about in a nice old horse-drawn *roman a clef* who would still be grievously shaken to see their own lineaments in a book by Henry Miller.

Like the censorship problem, with which it is inevitably entangled, the problems of infringement of self-esteem will undoubtedly go on proliferating through the pragmatic and piecemeal efforts we make to meet them. We may as well realize that it is not pre-eminently a question of infringing legal rights. In so far as literature is a healing or educational process, it takes as its own the riddles of such infringements. If anyone on earth is responsible, then fiction writers are pre-eminently responsible for understanding and explaining those violations of the person quite beyond the cognizance of the law. It is the limitless and everlasting job of the writer to query what is right, to guess at what is just, so that a part of his findings can be encoded sometime into law. The law can never lead.

Of course, in the confusions of the present, the novelist will think he hasn't much but brass and guts and common sense to guide him in those trespasses he commits on the lives around him. His great consolation may be that in the art of fiction— as in no other art I can think of—brass and guts and common sense show up as among the most valuable ingredients of his imagination. A novelist knows from the beginning that he is going to transgress. So, at least, he had better do it well. As Conrad says, "There is something after all in the world allowing one man to steal a horse while another must not look at a halter." What the novelist has most to be afraid of is not his transgressions, but being the wrong man to make them.

Homogenizing the Cows

The $20 million appropriated by Congress to back the government's program for the fine arts is a figure most artfully arrived at. It is a sum large enough to declare the affluence of the Great Society without palpably twitching the pocket of the individual taxpayer, costing General Dynamics a single contract, or keeping a single bomber out of the Asian sky.

What this money will do for the arts in our land is still partly conjectural, of course, though the guidelines for prediction were stated by Cyril Connolly 20 years ago: "Today the State shows a benevolent face to Culture-Diffusion, but to those who create culture no trace of sympathy or indulgence, with the result that we are becoming a nation of commentators, of critics and hack-explainers, most of whom are ex-artists. Everything for the Milk Bar, nothing for the Cow!"

The performing arts—as they were called when there was still a sensible distinction made between them and the arts of creation—stand to profit, first, most, and in cumulative progression of prestige from this infusion of federal money. According to the handwriting on the wall, the other arts will get their share in proportion to their success in pretending that they are performing arts, too. In recent years poetry has been going around in blackface, pretending by an emphasis on "readings" to be an occasion you could dress up and go to like the theater. (Ain't nobody here but us performing chickens, Mr. President.) And the art of painting *is* how many new galleries can be built on the new budget, how many lectures on appreciation can be scheduled, for through such programs more silver will trickle to more young men and women with paint brushes in their hands.

Forster used to admonish that "it's the inner life that counts," but a really astute analysis of the Pedernales culture pattern leads to this conclusion: It's the *outer inner* life that keeps faculty wives convinced we're hot on the trail of the Medicis.

I take this truth to be self-evident: that the Faculty Wife is to federal sponsorship of the arts what Mom is to the American military establishment, an imago without which the whole program would lose its orientation and wobble like a compass in a used-car dump. This orientation might have been different without the preparatory work of the foundations.

A dozen years ago when the Ford Foundation's money began to make itself felt, it appeared there might be a genuine Third Force emerging behind our arts and letters to check and balance the commercial art markets on the one hand and the bogy of bureaucratic prescription on the other. But with unerring instinct for the sure thing, the foundation plunked the bulk of its culture money on culture-diffusion projects designed to reassure the academic distaff it was not missing anything. By direct and indirect subsidization of what our ladies call "THUH Theater" the stewards of excess capital catered to a taste and a notion of culture given their definitive shape by the very bankruptcy the foundations were entrusted to redeem.

The foundation subsidized poets and novelists by "attaching" them to theater groups. The rationale behind this quaint displacement is impossible to find if we look for any conceivable benefit to poetry or fiction or any improvement of the audience for these arts. On the other hand, the public relations bonus for the theater and its adherents is as obvious as the kicker in a full color ad for a Mustang. "The poet Supplicore spent a year with the Okmulgee Group Theater, you know. Tried his hand on an experimental one-acter. Very interesting, but it wouldn't *play*." If well-talented Supplicore can't make it as playwright, that must mean that those who can, those who have made it writing the "literature of the theater," are real whizzes.

So runs the public-relations syllogism. *Ad majorem gloria* performing arts. Just as they are. Just as they were. Just as they shall be.

Instead of functioning as a countervailing power among the patrons and art consumers, the foundation has spent its bounty to create a cultural homogeneity where the very idea of checks and balances, of countervailing tendencies, has no more place than a rattrap in a cheese soufflé.

At this juncture the government picks up the tab of patronage. It is a government of the people, and the people, whatever their longing and ability, stand down along the garden paths where they've been led. Their representatives did not attain to office by championing the silent potential of popular longing against the chatter of The Thing That Works.

Inevitably the big slice of the people's $20 million will come back through the government for culture-diffusion. The big prestige that goes with big money will be adjusted to convince those who care that The Theater, The Orchestra, and The Dance are "Better Than Ever"—as they used to say about movies before movies became The Film. But strange things happen in the mill of the American government. It has ground small before this, when every preliminary sign was that it was going to throw out only lumps too big for digestion by the human craw.

May we rest confident that while the fiddles are playing and the dancers dancing and the directors directing and the faculty wives forgetting that when it's all over there'll still be the ride home in the four-year-old Chev and a Cub Scout shirt to iron before tomorrow's Den meeting and an interview with Representative Studge before the League of Women Voters *decides* —that very many young men and women will go on making undiffusable things of beauty?

And that the government, with all its might and majesty, the symbolic power represented by the emblematic bird on its coin, will well and truly endeavor to create, if not a whole culture, at least cases where the making of beautiful things shall be considered sufficient end for the investment of talent, breath, and taxes required to produce them?

Why I Left the Midwest

What are the facts of the case?

I was born in Cedar Falls, Iowa, and for forty-seven years of uneven patriotism I either insisted or permitted people to say that I was a midwesterner. Henceforth I will take pains to deny it.

Those are the facts, and they mean very little. Facts are what we can pick like blades of grass out of a field, selecting them and arranging them to fit whims of cowardice or bravery, our uglier compliances and even our lonely declarations of independence.

Realities are something else again. They twist us. As Whitehead declared in somewhat different language, realities are cloudy and indistinct to our perception, hard to articulate intelligibly, while facts, for whatever they are worth, are clear and sharp in outline. Almost any fact can be fitted into any supporting structure of assumption and verification. But the realities are what determine our choice of assumption and our choice to respect or repudiate the system of verification. And my present definition of myself and of my exile represents a rejection of the systems of verification which have come to dominate that mammoth, ill-defined, and willfully unself-conscious aggregate called the Midwest.

The fact may be that I was born in a bedroom in Cedar Falls, Iowa, while my parents were attending Iowa State Teachers College. The reality may be that they wanted to be educators because the Midwest of an earlier time showed them that was

a hopeful way to seek for the meaning of their lives—and that
they wasted their lives trying to cherish crumbs of hope from a
tide running out through decadence to despair. And that I—
who through their efforts and the efforts of individuals like
them—had a better chance to measure the scope of the tide than
they and was consequently obligated as much to the hopes that
sustained them as to the despair inherent in what I witnessed.

But between the facts and the reality, I remember this about
my birth: a flabby, sleepy little boy wearing overalls and a
summer shirt and tennis shoes, with a rayon beanie from the
dimestore on his head, was following a hay wagon along a hedge
row and over the crest of a hill on a farm three miles west of
Ash Grove, Iowa. The follower was a conglomerate of incomplete potentials for awareness, someone's child and someone's
brother, no doubt rather more solemn in appearance than was
in keeping with anything going on inside him. A little somebody, nobody, following an unpainted haywagon in the sleepi-
ness of a July afternoon, accepting the touch of breeze on his
skin without an inkling that the stir of his senses meant anything, without a suspicion that paths of light and sound and
gravity crossed at a decisive point within his nervous system,
forming a crossroads that might be either his or him.

Stubble and porous yellow clay were underfoot. The horses
Bird and Belle lunged amiably in their harness, leaving a dry
track and a faint, bright pennant of dust raised in the air by
the iron wagon wheels. A white-haired man swayed with the
wagon, a darker young man forked up the windrows of timothy
and grass. There was a gummy smell of hedge-trees and the
sweetly acrid smell of weeds untouched by the mower at the
field's edge but broken now by the wagon's passage.

Then there was pain.

I looked down. What had been a sweaty little chest under
someone's summer shirt was *mine,* and in the middle of my
chest, just above the bib of my overalls there was a rosy little
nipple of pain which could not be anybody else's. A hornet,
representing the state of Iowa and invested with the power of
the Midwest to call me to myself, had blundered inside my shirt
and stung me. Around that sharp tingling I had to admit my

existence as an independent entity distinguished from the patterns of sun, wind, hills, and fencerows as it was distinguished from the impalpable flow of heredity that had come into me from those two men gathering hay into the wagon. I was I because of them and the Midwest and the representative hornet, and by virtue of coming from such a combination into awareness, I always understood that henceforward any affirmations of belonging were the responsiblity of the self that could simultaneously *feel and see* the source of pain.

I am not going on to insist I was born of the Midwest that afternoon in the hayfield—there is much too much mystery about one's birth and origin and consequent loyalties for me to venture such a positive declaration. There is too much mystery about which facts open on a view of reality for me to risk either offending or amusing you by substituting the events that memory sustains for those useful, comfortable records kept in court house ledgers and elaborated through life by journalism, the military services, and the internal revenue bureau. I have recalled this episode in the hayfield merely to illustrate there is more than one sense to the statement that I was born in and of the Midwest. One is delivered again and again by the sting of self-awareness into . . . Well, into what? What is the right single term for labeling what one is born or delivered into? Into the "world"? Say the "world" if that is how it seems to you. I borrow a term from the poet Auden. "Out of the conservative dark, into the ethical life, the dense commuters come. . . ." One is delivered into the ethical life—the life where a conscious and responsible self meets others as, that afternoon in the hayfield, I first met my father when he walked back to see why I was hollering and whooping and waving my rayon beanie.

It seems to me I am speaking of reality when I say that I was born into the ethical life in and of the Midwest. In the candor of privacy, where proof is neither required nor relevant, I admit that all my notions of love and justice, the shape as well as the limitations of my sensibility were graven and determined for me by the Midwest that preceded them. So that in my chosen alienation from the Midwest as I find it now, I am choosing that alienation in the name of the Midwest that made me. When I say, "To hell with the Midwest"—and that, in so many flat words, is what I have chosen to say—I am saying it in the name of the Midwest. It would take a braver man than I to say such a thing because he had been hurt and stung, impoverished, ignored, or denied what his vanity supposes to be his rightful place in the sun by his region or his country. Those things can be accepted, and when they're not accepted as the normal tax on patriotism, clearly the fault is with the man who won't accept them, not in the country or region that imposes them.

I have been declaring myself—implicitly by my work and explicitly in more or less public statements, by the causes I've supported and by silences—an Iowa writer for some time— not to any great personal advantage, I might say, nor with any gratification to my vanity that I've been aware of. I never wanted, in so doing, to be a big frog in a small pool. That may be worth something, but it's not worth the pain of being stung by an Iowa hornet. If there had been, coming up in my generation, or among younger people, another, or several others who might more graciously or adequately define the role of the Iowa writer, I would or should have tried to declare that Iowa was better served by them than by me.

What I have found, instead of a proud identification by Iowa of these others with whom I would have gladly served, a collective denial of the very concept of an Iowa writer. Where are your writers, Iowa? Oh, there was so and so who is very successful and who was born in Iowa. Ah, there is such and such who uses Iowa material in a way that makes us proud to be Iowans. Oh, we have hired some respected professional writers—including yourself, don't forget—to teach in Iowa. . . .

Where are your young writers, emerging because their self-consciousness is yours, because their art, however crude, slow, unaccredited is a response to your yearning? Where are your young writers who have not yet been vouched for by the authorities to whom you have opened your culture market? Where are they?

And there is no answer to that in the whole state of Iowa, because such young writers are unthinkable. And if they are unthinkable, then that part of any of us which is most obligatory to defend—in the name of that which made it—is likewise unthinkable. Realizing that, one realizes the reality of his exile. And then it doesn't matter greatly whether one moves out physically or stays, the question is thereafter only one of expedience. But I think as we find ourselves among the unthinkables in the present Midwest, we have the duty to speak, as I am trying to speak now, to individuals of talent, promise, and hope, warning them that they cannot come to fulfillment and perhaps not to tolerable compromise with their frustrations in a climate where they are unthinkable.

I am not urging—I can't contemplate doing so—that the best young artists or writers of the Midwest ought to get out and go to New York, Majorca, San Francisco, or Australia. I am saying that for all that matters, they *have been* exiled by their native region, and if they want to re-enter it as respected, prosperous citizens who may, incidentally, practice an art, then the best way to expedite such re-entry is probably by going to New York and coming back with the spurious accreditation of the cultural capital.

Whether re-entry on such terms is worth working for is another question.

II

A few years ago that good midwesterner Alf Landon noted, "If you want to be heard in the Midwest, you have to go to the East and speak from there." I spent and shaped a large part of my life in the belief that this was an acceptable working formula for people like me as well as for politicians, though it obviously imposes a handicap and puts an extra tax on the endurance of those who have to make that longer trek alone.

The voice of the East, or from the East, will be heard in the Midwest, but there still remains the question: *Which* of the signals that altogether make up the message of the speaker will be heard and in what manner will the accepted signals be telling or effective?

Writing recently on the art centers and museums in the Midwest, the *New York Times* critic John Canaday said, "Most of these hopeful institutions are based on a saddening mis-conception—the idea that if a community can synthesize for itself some of the surface manifestations of culture, then culture will sink down from the top.

"Unfortunately this does not happen. Even the finest works of art have little value except as decorations or subjects for moony reveries unless they are understood as reflections of the culture that produced them. And they cannot create this aware-ness independently.

"The trouble with most small art museums is that they see their function as the appreciation and dissemination of some-thing called 'beauty' and this can get nobody anywhere."

The article from which I have quoted was reprinted in the Des Moines *Register* last summer, and that must indeed stand as some evidence that this sensible, crucial diagnosis from the East is being heard here where it counts. But then one reflects it may mean only further agonies of frustration for those out here who understand it best, as they find themselves unable to prevail against that strain in midwestern thinking which at best will note Dr. Canaday's findings in passing and then feel flat-tered to be the object of concern.

Without going to the extreme of taking public opinion polls on the question here raised, one can by simple inference realize that if Canaday is correct about the midwestern capacity for misprising and misunderstanding the role of the beautiful, by the same token and by the same mechanisms of distortion it is capable of ignoring common sense and wisdom, even when these, too, come from afar.

Undoubtedly some of you heard of the recent Carnegie Foundation report on the future of educational TV. In brief, this report recommends the use of regional and local television for the development of regional and local self-consciousness, in the arts, as I understand it, as well as in politics, business, and academic matters generally. The concerned midwesterner ought prayerfully to hope that what this eastern foundation recom-mends will come to pass. But how can he help wondering fearfully that when the showdown comes the Midwest will declare it has nothing to declare to itself—that it wants importations, imitations, what it believes to be the latest thing in more blessed regions like Hollywood and New York?

What is said, even from the East, may not *matter* to the Midwest. What is *heard* here will be determinative, and in the choice of what to hear, neither Solomon nor John Canaday, Christ or the Carnegie Foundation will be of any help.

In one of my lesser attempts to address the Midwest from the vantage of a New York address I wrote a letter to the editor of the Des Moines *Register* enclosing a clipping from a New York *Post* column by Murray Kempton. Somewhat playfully but nonetheless clearly Mr. Kempton averred that the Iowa women he had seen when he accompanied Chairman Kruschchev on his visit to the state looked like horse's asses. I admit a cloudy mixture of motives in my attempt to call this aspersion to the attention of my native state through the letters-to-the-editor column. I might be able to reconstruct them in detail, but perhaps it will suffice now to say they were experimental. For my own soul's sake I was testing again whether I should choose to or *could* call myself an Iowan.

The results, as with many of the experiments we make in our search for the realities, only embroiled me deeper in the question. The *Register* simply did not notice or print this communication to them. Of course that was proof of nothing important, but it was the opening for me of a new branch of speculation about what it is that the Midwest is listening for in the voices from the East. My incomplete investigation of what will be heard and unheard in the Midwest suggests it will choose to hear the *note of concern* expressed by John Canaday and the Carnegie Corporation, it will respond with noisy outbursts of unconvincing dismay at flippant articles like the one Philip Roth published a few years ago in *Esquire,* but will resolutely and deafly ignore suggestions that those who supply it with cultural models and fads of liberal political thought might be contemptuous of it for welcoming them.

If the dangerous cutting edge of Dr. Canaday's diagnosis should, for an example, slip through the guard of complacent misinterpretation—if the administrators of culture in the Midwest should be shocked to admit, "Why, he means us!"—then I suppose they would shop for another doctor with a more consoling prognosis. In the progress of every terminal disease there must be a period in which despair of remedy becomes, in itself, a contributary morbid factor. If the patient is wealthy, as the Midwest certainly is now, and as it will be increasingly, then the temptation is all the stronger to shop for the consolation of quacks—academic and commercial entrepreneurs of culture whose advice amounts to this: If you are blind, let me sell you some new eyeballs.

Those tormented individuals in the Midwest—and I hope somewhat cruelly that I am including all of you when I speak of the tormented—who still can see what is going on, must see that year by year the frantic lurch of the Midwest to keep up with New York in the arts is becoming more acute. Where the cry is for culture, is it not a cry for an Andy Warhol in every Kansas town, for "happenings" on the village green like those in Greenwich Village, for the *avant garde,* the *avant garde,* whether or not the guard advances from anything real, familiar, or even known to the Midwest?

In the national press a few years ago there were stories of the young man elected president of the student body of Iowa State University at Ames. He must have struck New York readers as being rather pathetically behind the times with his beat generation antics and already antiquated slogans of revolt. But, we read, "he is going to drag Iowa kicking and screaming into the twentieth century." As if the twentieth century for Iowa could be somehow preciously experienced by a popularization of styles and slogans taken over from the cosmopolitan discard. Perhaps he was in favor of thinking seriously about LSD and believed that if all Iowans thought seriously about it they would then "enter the twentieth century."

And such young frauds, proliferating successfully across the midwestern scene, will be accepted as "the opposition" to a crusty old guard of midwestern reactionaries. They are no such thing. They are no more and no less than a symptom of the illusions about itself that the Midwest is content to buy up in the days of its affluence. The real radicals, the true hopes, the young born into the ethical life with capacities for art and other responsibilities, belong neither with the fake rebels nor the complacent sojourners.

Here one must note another phase of the vicious circle. Accelerated to its present velocity, it will be accelerated further by the flight or withdrawal into interior exile of its best young people. It has become almost the measure of their talent and courage that they will recognize the processes I am beginning to describe. And as they do, they will use the educational and cultural accommodations that affluence provides—not as the beginning of a career in and a dialogue with the Midwest that stung them into existence. But as a means of escaping from it. Of getting out.

Through the years of my life in and out of the Midwest, I have had some very minor active part in it, none of which I will cite, because in my effort to speak of realities none of my part is worth citing except my role as observer. A role which, I suppose, is played by observation of oneself in relation to the general processes and not by detached or sociological measurements of mass movements.

I never knew myself by any neat label of writer, teacher, citizen, taxpayer, citizen, lecturer, soldier, gadfly, or agitator. I knew myself as a man who was obligated by his talents and experiences—whatever they might be worth on an objective scale—to raise his voice and cry to the Midwest, "Hear me, O Israel." I had something to say, not because of any purely personal merits, but because something had been said to me. By the Midwest. By voices and places and dignities that were not mine, but which I might aspire to echo and pass on.

I saw myself thus. But in the distorting mirror that the Midwest offered me in recent years, I saw reflected the pig who had been, not very gloriously, after all, to the culture market in New York, valued or ignored on the basis of his market value, his voice lost somewhere on the wind. And no loyalty can very long survive the great shame of seeing oneself in these irreconcilable images.

III

The decadence of the Midwest might be represented as resulting from demographic and technological circumstances, shifts in the balance of those powers that always influence and sometimes determine the tone of a culture. No one will be moved to action by any such findings. Objective studies of the Midwest, its investments in culture and its penetration by the media of communication, will never satisfy any of us in his privacy when he confronts questions of loyalty and hope. What angers and frightens me is the spirit in which the Midwest accepted what was being done to it. What flaw made it insist on debating false alternatives?

Was the choice really between provincialism and cosmopolitanism? Was it between conservativism and progressivism? Between local chauvinism and boundaryless globalism?

None of us wanted to live in a provincial Midwest, deaf and blind to the intellectual adventures, the discoveries and anguishes of the rest of the world. When I was young in college in Iowa, going up to Chicago had a special value and glamour, because Chicago was our own place to meet the world. I remember standing in the grand Chicagoey gloom of the Art Institute in front of Van Gogh's painting of Dr. Gachet's garden, stung in the breast and fighting for my life. The hot days of Dakota and all the blades of fevered vegetation that jangled in the sun over Iowa seemed balanced and reflected by what, in the painting, had come from far off. The painting was foreign and familiar at once because I had been given something by the Midwest to confront it with.

I was young and drunk in Chicago in the nights on the Near North Side and we were in studios and bar, talking about Hitler and Picasso, that wandering midwesterner Hemingway and the wandering Irishman Joyce, and one night I was sitting drunk under a grand piano in a studio apartment near the water tower while some of the crowd read a play by Gertrude Stein. Miss Stein was not of our province, not Midwest, but to hear her quirky words there was a midwestern experience, the kind of thing defined in Whitman's wonderful little poem on Italian music in the Dakotas—"strangely fitting even here, meanings unknown before."

If we remember we are in Dakota, only then do the meanings unknown before emerge from the art works and the wisdom imported from Italy or Paris or New York. To ignore the foreignness of the foreign may be a posture of cosmopolitanism, but a lack of self-awareness means, in the long or short run, a diminishment of awareness that other selves exist, that the world of culture is a world of men, not of beautiful objects. As, in the ethical life, we can approach justice only by an assertion of our individuality among other individualities.

The question is never what is *best* in art or conduct, but always what is *best for us*. *Politically* the question for the Midwest was never really whether progressivism or conservatism was best. That may not finally matter. However the Midwest falls short of discovering its natural political posture and conceiving a broadly human end to approach, its conservatism will be selfish and mean, its progressivism reckless and irresponsible.

When I used to hear the Midwest berated or ridiculed for its isolation, I brooded loyally with the hope that this isolationism had some historic purpose that might in time emerge. It seemed to me that the region was biding its time like Grant in Galena—to quote a passage from that midwesterner F. Scott Fitzgerald. That it was modestly, powerfully preparing to offer virtues that had ripened in patience. But the political complexion of the Midwest has changed in the time since the war with no sign that the old conservativism deepened, enriched, or ripened the new progressivism. And when one fears that the long-term threat to democracy is from an engineered consensus, one specifies that a prime ingredient for such control is a numerical majority of docile voters against which no passion or reason of any minority can make headway. And fears that the destiny of the Midwest is merely to swell that dehumanized majority. It may indeed be rash of me to prophesy such a destiny for the Midwest. It would be more rash to stay when I see it implacably emerging.

I used to take a sombre, subterranean, patriotic delight in identifying with such uncomfortable Midwestern heroes as John

L. Lewis, the architect and chief of the UMW. When he quoted Shakespeare in some of his epic, headlined battles, that struck me as a midwestern thing to do—particularly considering the quotes he selected. Once with midwestern scorn he quoted a contemptuous passage declaring he would not "crook the pregnant hinges of the knee where thrift may follow fawning." In its independence and defiance and confidence in values beyond the immediate show of things, he made the passage sound simultaneously Shakespearean and midwestern. And when he bellowed, "O, it is great to have a giant's strength, but to use it like a giant is tyrannous," I think no one mistook this for an attempt at cosmopolitanism on his part. It was borrowed to assert that a real and not a sham pluralism was the essence of America. This pluralism could be and was a reality as long as major segments of the republic, like the Midwest, could join in a congress with others without submerging identity in an amorphous single mass.

That was in another time. Lewis is gone and those who will quote Shakespeare or Milton's "known rules of ancient liberty" or anything else without being assured from afar that it's cool to do so, are gone. The Midwest was a great part of the human dream. But a bitter Greek challenged, "Praise the day in the evening."

In this twilight of democracy, in the vilest hour of American history, doesn't the Midwest see, in the figure of Lyndon Johnson, with his shallow, clichéd pieties, his show of bustling energy, his slippery, cunning debasement of language, the incarnation of itself—the inflated and now ominous composite of Sinclair Lewis figures that has bided its time in the shadows, emerging at last to shock the disbelieving world with its cry, "We have got what they want and they are trying to take it away from us." A slogan which, in its untempered crudeness, sounds like a warrant for taking arms against every hungry man on earth.

There has lately been much talk of the arrogance of power. This charge will fly over the head of the Midwest, where there has never been much arrogance. Truly not. But we from the Midwest know—we have always known, though we have contrived to suppress our knowledge—a secret more deadly to humanity than the arrogance of power. What we knew, what we were nursing under our conservatism and amoral diffidence, was that the giant brute of mass man can commit itself to pure and purposeless power without the minimal redeeming grace, the touch of pride, in the glamour of arrogance.

When I was very young, with my family I used to go up from the very small towns that we called home to Des Moines to the state fair. I remember from very far back the cow sculptured in butter, the absolutely enchanting smells of fruit mingling with flower smells in the airy hall where apples, pears, peaches, cherries, and grapes competed for agricultural prizes. The smell of popcorn, dust, and automobile exhaust among the flags and advertisements. And over the sights and smells of the fair I read, painted on the wall of one or another of the public buildings, this sign: *Where there is no vision the people perish.*

I don't say I was much impressed by the sign then or by its sense. I gawked at it and, as you see, it stuck in my memory along with a million other incoherent impressions of my home state and region. But as one grows older and willy-nilly reads the pattern traced in the flux of experience, one reads coherences invisible before. One goes on reading words encountered first in contexts to which they had no overwhelming relevance. At last I read the words as a warning with a very personal application. Coupled with my instinct for survival, the sign said, *"Homo fugit.* Get out while you can!"

In my last year in Iowa I took part in what might be called an Iowa-style great debate at the university—"Iowa-style" meaning it was full of slyness, uncertainty, bluff goodwill, treachery, yearning, coercions never admitted, and appeals to old loyalties. At the end of this great debate when I had already made arrangements to move and to withdraw my manuscripts from the University of Iowa library, I had a little conference with a high administrative official of the university.

I said that though I was leaving, I felt both a wish and an obligation to explain my ultimate view of what was taking place there. In somewhat different terms with different instances I told him what I have said here. I said I had been in opposition to those who thought that since the legislature was getting more "liberal" they could now buy for Iowa a better place in the cultural sun.

He said he was sorry that Iowa had disappointed me.

I said that expediency, political maneuvering, jockeying for personal advantage had prevented any clear articulation of the issues most important to the students and the concerned people of the state.

He said that since I had written a novel about academic politics I should understand how that happened.

I said I had meant to write a novel about education.

He nodded, Yes. Same thing.

Then with a flick of his wrists and impatience in his tone, he said, "If you feel the way you do, why don't you take your manuscripts and just GO-ooh!"

I took my manuscripts and I went.

This book was set in Baskerville type face with chapter headings in Caslon. The letterpress printing was done by C. E. Pauley and Company, Indianapolis, Indiana, on 70 lb. Warren's Old Style paper. Binding in Interlaken cloth was done at the Modern Binding Corporation, Portland, Indiana. The jacket was designed by Dan Estes, Purdue University designer, and printed by offset lithography by the Metropolitan Printing Service, Bloomington, Indiana. Editorial and production supervision were by Eleanor Crandall and Diane Dubiel.

DATE DUE

FEB 4 1970			
GAYLORD			PRINTED IN U.S.A.